DHTML
LEARNING
BY EXAMPLE

Robert B. Mellor
IT University of Copenhagen

Franklin, Beedle & Associates, Inc.
8536 SW St. Helens Drive, Suite D
Wilsonville, OR 97070
503-682-7668
www.fbeedle.com

President and Publisher	Jim Leisy (jimleisy@fbeedle.com)
Production	Stephanie Welch
Manuscript Editor	Dean Lake
Proofreader	Tom Sumner
Cover Design	Ian Shadburne
Marketing	Christine Collier
Order Processing	Krista Brown

Library of Congress cataloging-in-publication data is available from the publisher.

CONTENTS

PREFACE

DHTML: Learning by Example describes briefly and in plain language the elements and attributes in HTML and shortly compares the 3.2 and 4 versions of HTML to XHTML. The Microsoft Document Object Model (DOM) is then introduced, where elements are considered to be objects. The CSS hierarchical model is explored using HTML and XML examples, followed by client-side scripting using JavaScript and VBScript. Finally, the last third of the book illustrates "Dynamic Scripting," the combination of CSS, DOM, and JavaScript.

    This book contains 26 examples, along with many other coding illustrations, with each followed by a detailed explanation. Theory, tips, and new concepts are introduced along the way, both in the body of the text, as well as in the examples. Experience shows quite clearly that if you sit down at your PC and read/work through the book, you will be able to do most DHTML programming within a few days. The code for all the Examples can be downloaded from the publishers web site (**www.fbeedle.com/83-x.html**).

For this work you will ideally have a 4+ version Internet Explorer browser (MSIE4+) from Microsoft. This is available free from microsoft.com (**http://www.microsoft.com**). For Example D you will need a 5+ version Internet Explorer browser; however, it can be displayed in Internet Explorer 4 if you add the XML parser (called "msxml"), which is available free from microsoft.com (**http://msdn.microsoft.com/downloads/webtechnology/xml/ msxml.asp**). This is the only example where you will need an XML-enabled browser.

You will need a graphics program in order to make some simple GIF files. The Windows program MS-Paint is sufficient. If you have others, like Adobe Photoshop version 4+ or Corel Draw, you will not need their more advanced features.

An ASCII text editor is sufficient to write the code examples described in this book. The program Notepad (under Windows accessories—or if you prefer you can download the freeware EditPad from Tucows.com) can easily be used in conjunction with Windows Explorer and Microsoft Internet Explorer. All HTML programmers have a shortcut to Notepad or EditPad on the graphical interface (command/right click on Notepad, make a shortcut, then left-click and drag the shortcut out to the working surface, the "desktop"). Open NotePad and write the HTML code. Save the file with the extension .htm or html. Find it again in Windows Explorer and double-click it. It should open in Microsoft

Internet Explorer. Most programmers then work with two windows open, Notepad and Microsoft Internet Explorer. Simply write more in Notepad, save, then refresh in Microsoft Internet Explorer. There are many more sophisticated ways of programming HTML. One very nice program is HomeSite. HomeSite 1.2 used to be available free from **www.dexnet.com**, and the more advanced 4.5 version can be bought from **www.allaire.com**. FrontPage Express is included in many Microsoft Office versions, and Netscape Composer is available for those with Corel Office packages. The most commonly used WYSIWYG (what you see is what you get) HTML editors are FrontPage and Macromedia Dreamweaver, but the expression WYSIWYG should be used with caution here. What you have made is not always what other people see! For this book you should keep it simple, and just use an ASCII or very simple HTML editor and a 4+ version browser, preferably Internet Explorer.

This book covers the basics of CSS and JavaScript 1.1 & 1.2, referring only to JScript where there are significant deviations. Other scripting languages, like VBScript and Active Server Pages, are touched upon only very briefly and the interested reader is referred to my book *ASP: Learning by Example*. Likewise, more detailed explanations about eXtensible Markup Language (XML, XSL and XHTML) can be found in my book *XML: Learning by Example*. The interested reader is also referred to further readings on these subjects in the list of web links in Appendix E.

The Author

Dr. Robert B. Mellor teaches at the IT University of Copenhagen. He has 16 years of teaching experience in several countries and is an examiner at many universities all over the world.

Symbols and Conventions

In this book text written in `Courier` represents code. New terms are introduced in *italics*. There should not be line breaks in JavaScript scripting code when written in your editor. CSS code can be broken, but it is recommended to keep each statement on one line for ease of reading. If in doubt, download the codes from the web support at **www.fbeedle.com/83-x.html**.

DHTML

What is DHTML? Nobody can buy a software pack called DHTML and install it on their PC. DHTML (Dynamic HTML) is rather the name given to a set of possibilities that make client-side Internet programming more interactive. There are international standards for DHTML—called Document Object Model (DOM)—but Netscape Navigator 4 was marketed before these were published, with the result that Netscape Navigator 4 supports the majority of the "standard properties," as well as some others that are unique to Netscape Navigator 4. Conversely, Microsoft's IE4 came on the market later, and supports a package called MS Dynamic HTML Object Model, which not only supports all of the basic DOM, but also goes much further.

What is called "DHTML" consists of HTML 4, JavaScript/JScript/ECMA Common Standard, plus Cascading Style Sheets (CSS), the MS Dynamic HTML Object Model, as well as the Microsoft-specific VBScript/ActiveX Controls. DHTML is part of the general computing trend of the 1990s, the tendency away from structured programming, with a focus on actions (like verbs in our language), and toward object-based programming (OOP—Object Oriented Programming), where the objects can be compared to nouns in our language. Obviously, it is easier to speak a language containing both verbs and nouns!

Apart from the above, many effects seen "out on the net" are made using Java 2 (Java Applets). Java is a separate programming language. It should not be confused with JavaScript, and it is not considered to be part of DHTML.

When an Internet file is "hit" by a client, the file is written to cache and viewed in the browser program. MSIE5 converts every element in that document into an object. Objects have properties and are able to perform functions (their *methods*). Using scripting languages (like JavaScript), commands can be written which change an object's properties and/or force them to execute various functions without re-loading (or re-downloading) the file. This is the essence of "client-side" programming.

THE VARIOUS HTMLS AND XHTML

In classical HTML (HTML 3.2), *tags*, like <p>, open and close with *delimiters* (< >). For example:

```
<p>this is text in paragraph tags</p>
```

The whole of this, from the opening delimiter (<) of the first tag, to the last delimiter (>) of the closing tag, is called an *element*. Elements can have *attributes*. Attributes are written into the opening tag thus:

```
<p align="center">this text is now centered</p>
```

where the alignment attribute is set using a single equals (=) sign, to the value "center", which is rendered in double quotation marks (").

This is fine for most uses, but let us assume you have 6,000 HTML files, each containing three to five horizontal lines like this:

```
<hr bgcolor="blue" height="2" width="80%">
```

Quite obviously it is a tedious task to check each Horizontal Ruler (hr) tag to see that you have written it properly. Thus HTML 4 puts much less weight on writing attributes in elements by expressly giving the programmer the possibility to define attributes centrally. This tendency is extended when using XML, where attributes within tags are almost (but not quite, see below) completely dropped, and their position is taken by *name-spaces* (see my book, *XML: Learning by Example*).

Thus, in HTML 4 one may write:

```
<style>
.bigblue {font-family:Arial; font-size=12; color=blue}
</style>
<body>
<p CLASS=bigblue>This text is big and blue</p>
```

Here you can see that the element has no immediate attributes, but is being regarded by the browser as an *object*. Objects have *properties,* which in this case are referred to using CLASS and bundled under the description bigblue. What exactly is contained in the description bigblue is defined in this case within <style> tags in the documents head.

In HTML 4, properties and attributes can be mixed. For example:

```
<p CLASS=bigblue align=center>This text is big and blue and
centered</p>
```

HTML 4 saves work because the programmer does not have to define attributes (or at least not all attributes) in each element, but rather central or repeating motifs can simply be defined in Cascading Style Sheets (CSS). In XML, both CSS and XSL (eXtensible Stylesheet Language) can be used (see *XML: Learning by Example*).

From the above it can be seen that HTML 3.2 demands double quotes (") around the attribute value. HTML 4 leaves this open for the programmer, except where the attribute value contains a space, a situation where double quotes are demanded in HTML 4. Either with or without are typically accepted, but the beginner is advised to not mix 3.2 and 4 styles, but rather to stick to one style, preferably using double quotes, to be HTML 3.2 compatible (and XHTML compatible, see below). Note that mixing can easily lead to improper tags like:

```
<p align="center>
```

which will simply return an error!

However, both HTML 3.2 and HTML 4 allow tags to be written in either upper or lower case:

`<p></p>` or

`<P></P>` or

`<P></p>` or

`<p></P>`

are all interpreted as identical and correct. Furthermore, tags can overlap:

`<p>without<b> bold<i> italics </b> or just italics</p></i>`

In HTML these "bad habits" with mixing elements, forgetting to close tags, etc., are permitted. Browser software has grown to enormous proportions because the browser must be able to correctly interpret imprecise code. Handheld devices like PalmPilots and WAP phones do not have the storage memory for large browsers, so XML and applications like XHTML and WML (Wireless Markup Language, a part of WAP, Wireless Applications Protocol) have to be written strictly.

To repeat this important difference: In contrast to HTML (3.2 or 4), when using XHTML (or XML), a tag opens, then any nested tags are included and closed (or *escaped*, like `<IMG SRC="1.gif" />`, or if they are empty, like `<br />`) before the first tag closes, whereupon the next tag opens. CSS and DHTML techniques are highly relevant to XHTML, therefore, because XML and XHTML are commonly regarded as the future of the Internet, it is a good idea to start being strict now.

XHTML stands for eXtensible HTML, but it could just as easily stand for "eXact HTML." XHTML is an XML-simplified and XML-compatible version of HTML. It demands an exact syntax (just as XML does) due to the increasing demand for small devices; you simply cannot install Internet Explorer 5 or Netscape 6 onto your mobile phone.

XHTML tags are similar to HTML tags with some exceptions:

- All XHTML tags must be in lowercase.

- All start tags must have a corresponding end tag.

- Empty tags are terminated by *escaping* (slash sign, /) within the delimiters, e.g., `<br />`. An extra white space may be included (increases compatibility with older browsers).

- Overlapping tags are not permitted, and apparent overlaps have to be nested, e.g., `<p><font><i>` followed by `</i></font></p>`, in that order.

- Attribute values must appear in quotes and may not be minimized, e.g., `<hr noshade>` becomes `<hr noshade="noshade" />`.

However, the use of capital letters in the tags in this book are for pedagogical purposes only.

CASCADING STYLE SHEETS—CSS

This section focuses on Cascading Style Sheets (CSS), especially when used as external source (.css) files. CSS allows us to sharply define the difference between a web documents structure (layout, design, etc.) and its information content.

CSS contains the possibility of defining the various properties (color, size, etc.) of the various elements (paragraph, P; anchor, A, etc.) in a document. There are three ways of specifying CSS:

- *Inline*: Exactly where it is needed.

- *Declared*: In a <STYLE></STYLE> block in <HEAD>.

- *External*: In a separate file.

Example A: Inline Style

1. Open your HTML or ASCII editor and type:

```
<HTML>
<HEAD>
</HEAD>
<BODY>
<p>here is some text without Style</p>
<p style = "font-size: 20pt">text in 20 pt</p>
<p style = "font-size: 30pt; color: #0000FF">text in 30 pt</p>
</BODY>
</HTML>
```

2. Save the file as A.htm and open it in your browser.

Explanation

In <BODY>, a paragraph without Style is first defined (opened) then closed. In the following two paragraphs Style is defined immediately after opening the P tag. Here font-size is defined, followed by a colon (:) sign and which size, in points (pt), the font should be. Notice the Style stops when the defined element—that particular paragraph—is closed </P>. In the third paragraph, the font Style is *concatenated* using the semicolon (;) sign, which allows us to specify many properties in one Style declaration.

Example B: Declared Style in the Style Element

1. Open your HTML or ASCII editor and type:

```
<HTML>
<HEAD>
<style type="text/css">
```

```
EM {background-color: red; color: white}
H1 {font-family: Arial}
P  {font-size: 18pt}
.blue {color: blue}
</style>
</HEAD>
<BODY>
<H1 class="blue">Title</H1>
<p>Text Text Text Text Text Text Text Text Text</p>
<H1>Title 2<H1>
<p class = "blue">more Text more Text more Text<em> more Text
in italics</em>more Text<em>italic text again</em></p>
</BODY>
</HTML>
```

2. Save the file as B.htm and open it in your browser.

Explanation

Here in <HEAD> a new element <STYLE> is opened and its MIME-Type specified (text/css). Other types can be text/html, text/javascript, or image/gif. Afterwards, the various elements are specified, each within a curly brace { }, encasing the properties they should have. These are called *selectors* and serve to bind the style rule to a subset of elements in the document. In the example, EM (italic) text should be rendered in white and the Style is concatenated with a background color, red. Notice that this definition applies not to one specific EM block, but to all. Header 1 (H1) is defined as being in the font-family Arial, and text within <P> is defined as being 18pt.

Here the concept of Class is introduced (*Class selectors*). Class is an identification tag where the properties defined apply to that element. Class must not be confused with ID. *ID selectors* will be presented later. Each Class has a name, and here it is called `blue`. It is defined in <STYLE> without the word "Class," instead using only a full stop (a dot, `.`), i.e. `.blue`. The full stop is not used when the Class is called (i.e., `class="blue"`, not `class=".blue"`). A Class can be used in several different elements (here in both H1 and in P).

When an element is placed inside an element it is called a *Child* element of a *Parent* element, and simple "inheritance" rules apply. Therefore, in EM (a Child element of P in the example) the text is 18 point (this is simply inherited), but is not blue, although in the Parent P `Class="blue"`. This is because Child rules are thought to be more specific, and therefore take priority.

Example C: Linked External Style Sheets

Here, Style definitions are made in a separate file and copied by means of a reference link to the <HEAD> of each document. This is very useful in web sites where all files should have an identical, template-like layout.

1. Open your HTML or ASCII editor and type:

```
A {text-decoration:none}
A:hover{text-decoration:underline;  color:red;
background-color: #CCFFCC}
LI EM {color:red; font-weight: bold}
UL {margin-left: 2cm}
UL UL {text-decoration: underline; margin-left: .5cm}
```

2. Save the document as C.css, then open your HTML or ASCII editor again and type:

```
<HTML>
<HEAD>
<link rel="stylesheet" type="text/css" href="C.css">
```

```
</HEAD>
<BODY>
<H1>Shopping list for <em>Monday</em></H1>
<UL>
<LI>Milk</LI>
<LI>Bread
<UL>
<LI>Pita bread</LI>
<LI>Black bread</LI>
<LI>French baguettes</LI>
</UL></LI>
<LI>Rice</LI>
<LI>Potatoes</LI>
<LI>Pizza <em>with pepperoni</em></LI>
</UL>
<a href="http://www.an_url.com/theoretical/grocersshop/">
Order here</a>
</BODY>
</HTML>
```

2. Save the file as C.htm and open it in your browser.

Explanation

In the document's <HEAD> there is a *Link Element*:

```
<link rel="stylesheet" type="text/css" href="C.css">
```

Using *Relationship* (rel), the link specifies what type of relationship exists between the calling document, and that which is specified at the given (href) location, including its MIME type. Thus the text contained in the file C.css is read in as if it had been written there. Various Styles for various elements (Undefined List/UL, Anchor/A, etc.) are specified there and become "active" in C.htm.

THE "CASCADE" IN CASCADING STYLE SHEETS

It is already quite clear that conflicts can arise in Style, either deliberately or not. Conflicts are "settled" by a cascading hierarchy in three parts:

1. The Parent/Child type of conflict seen in Example B. Here the Child will take over the "inheritance" of the Parent, unless there is a conflict, in which case the Child rules take priority.

2. Conflicts arising between Styles specified in External, Declared, and Inline Styles. In this case, again the most specific takes priority, so Inline specifications take priority over all others, Declared Styles takes priority over External only, and External is the "weakest," having the lowest priority of all.

3. Other conflicts are resolved using the order in which the rules are specified as the document is read into the browser.

CSS allows us to position elements using the Position property in the capacities of Absolute Positioning and Relative Positioning.

Example D: Linked External CSS in XML

For this example you will need a 5+ version Internet Explorer browser; however, it can be displayed in Internet Explorer 4 if you add the XML parser (called "msxml"), which is available free from microsoft.com (**http://msdn.microsoft.com/downloads/ webtechnology/xml/msxml.asp**). This is the only example where you will need an XML-enabled browser.

In this example we will make two files, an XML file (D.xml) and the corresponding style source file (D.css).

1. Open your ASCII editor and type:

```
<?xml-stylesheet type="text/css" href="D.css"?>
<document>
<body>
<warning>beware of warnings </warning>
conversely
<tip>welcome any tips </tip>
and
<resource>and use your resources</resource>
</body>
</document>
```

2. Save the document as D.xml, and then in a new document type:

```
tip {background-color:green;}
resource {background-color:blue;}
warning {background-color:red;}
```

3. Save this document as D.css.

4. Open D.xml in your browser.

Explanation

As in all XML documents, the start tag contains <, ?, and xml. The declaration continues to refer to data presentation (style), the MIME type, and URL of the code source. Although the purpose here is not to explain XML, it can be seen that the "root element" has been called document. This contains a nested element body, which in turn contains three non-overlapping child elements. The assignment of names to the elements is not relevant (indeed, they could have been the proverbial Tom, Dick, and Harry. That is the eXtensible part of XML). What is important is that:

- They are not HTML tags.

- They correspond with the assignments defined in D.css.

Example D functions as seen in Example C; however, it is important to note that CSS will recognize well-formed tags, even when they are not HTML tags. This illustrates that CSS is a tool usable beyond the limits of HTML.

Example E: Absolute Positioning

1. Make two small image (.gif) files called 1.gif and 2.gif, then open your HTML or ASCII editor and type:

```
<HTML>
<HEAD>
</HEAD>
<BODY>
<IMG src="1.gif" style="position: absolute; top:0px;
left:0px; z-index:1">
<H1 style="position: absolute; top:50px; left:50px;
z-index:3">
<IMG src="2.gif" style="position: absolute; top:25px;
left:100px; z-index:2">
</BODY>
</HTML>
```

2. Save this document as E.htm.

3. Open E.htm in your browser.

Explanation

Here the Parent element is <BODY>, so the positions referred to for the element IMG (with the source the appropriate .gif file) are 0 pixels (px) from the left side and 0 pixels from the top. Positioning right and bottom are also allowed. If the elements (in this case the two pictures) should overlap, then the one specified first in the document is shown on top, unless z-index is specified. z-index is the "third dimension" (after X and Y) and specifies which order in a "stack" that element should be shown. The greater the z-index the higher the element; i.e., that element with the highest z-index is shown below all others. z-index is detailed further in Example T.

Example F: Relative Positioning

1. Open your HTML or ASCII editor and type:

```
<HTML>
<HEAD>
<STYLE TYPE="text/css">
p {font-size:15; font-family:Verdana}
span {color:red; font-size:10}
.super {position:relative; top:-1ex}
.sub { position:relative; bottom:-1ex }
.shift1 { position:relative; left:-1ex }
.shift2 { position:relative; right:-1ex }
</STYLE>
</HEAD>
<BODY>
<P>
Text Text Text <span class="super">superscript</span>
<br>Text Text Text <span class="sub">subscript</span>
```

```
<br>Text Text Text <span class="shift1"> Left </span>Text
Text Text.
<br>Text Text Text <span class="shift2"> Right </span>
Text Text Text.
</P>
</BODY>
</HTML>
```

2. Save the file as F.htm and open it in your browser.

Explanation

In this example the positioning is relative. Therefore, the page layout is determined using <P>, so the Parent element is Paragraph, and the inline elements are oriented according to that.

<span> is a *generic group element* shown inline without any special format and is used to attach an identity (in this example, class) to text or other elements. Span is similar to DIV, except that DIV is a *block level element* and, as such, is shown on a new line and has margins.

Example G: Background Color and Background Graphics

CSS can be used for both background color and also background graphics. Here you will need to make an appropriate GIF file (in this example called choose_a.gif).

1. Open your HTML or ASCII editor and type:

```
<HTML>
<HEAD>
<STYLE TYPE="text/css">
body {background-image: url(choose_a.gif);
background-position:top right; background-repeat:no-repeat;
background attachment:fixed}
```

```
</STYLE>
</HEAD>
<BODY>
<P>
blank Text blank Text blank Text blank Text blank Text
blank Text blank Text blank Text blank Text blank Text
blank Text blank Text blank Text blank Text blank Text
blank Text blank Text blank Text blank Text blank Text
blank Text blank Text blank Text blank Text blank Text
blank Text blank Text blank Text blank Text blank Text
blank Text blank Text blank Text blank Text blank Text
blank Text blank Text blank Text blank Text blank Text
blank Text blank Text blank Text blank Text blank Text
blank Text blank Text blank Text blank Text blank Text
blank Text blank Text
</P>
</BODY>
</HTML>
```

2. Save the file as G.htm and open it in your browser.

Explanation

Background-position determines the pictures position on the page using top, bottom, center, left or right, either alone or in combination. Where the picture is positioned is given using:

`Background-position:50% 30px`

where horizontal is given first (in this case 50%, i.e., centered), followed by vertical (in this case 30px). Clearly, % or px can be used in either case. `background-repeat` determines both where and how often a picture is repeated. The default value is simply `repeat`, but `no-repeat`, `repeat-x`, or `repeat-y` are possible (repeat not, or horizontally, or vertically). `background-attachment` has either the values of `fixed` (the picture stays put) or `scroll` (the picture scrolls up and down "attached" to the text).

Example H: Element Dimensions

1. Open your HTML or ASCII editor and type:

```
<HTML>
<HEAD>
<STYLE TYPE="text/css">
DIV {background-color: #FFCCFF}
</STYLE>
</HEAD>
<BODY>
<P>BackGround Text BackGround Text BackGround Text
BackGround Text BackGround Text BackGround Text
BackGround Text BackGround Text BackGround Text
BackGround Text BackGround Text BackGround Text

<DIV style="float:right; background-color: #FFCCFF">This Text
is put in using "float" in the DIV which forces other Text to
"move over" and make room for it. The opposite of "float" is
"clear"</DIV>

BackGround Text BackGround Text BackGround Text
BackGround Text BackGround Text BackGround Text
BackGround Text BackGround Text BackGround Text
BackGround Text BackGround Text BackGround Text
BackGround Text BackGround Text BackGround Text
BackGround Text
</p>
```

```
<DIV style="width: 20%">First   Text First   Text First   Text
First   Text First   Text First   Text First   Text First   Text
First   Text First   Text First   Text First </DIV><br><br>

<DIV style="width:80%; text-align:center">This Text is shown
in 80% of the DIV This Text is shown in 80% of the DIV This
Text is shown in 80% of the DIV This Text is shown in 80% of
the DIV This Text is shown in 80% of the DIV</DIV>

<!-text-align values can be either Left or Right -->
<br><br>
<DIV style="width:30%; height:10%; overflow:scroll">This Text
is only 30% of the DIV windows width, and if there is more
text than can be shown, then the DIV window gets scroll bars.
This Text is only 30% of the DIV windows width, and if there
is more text than can be shown, then the DIV window gets
scroll bars. </DIV>
</BODY>
</HTML>
```

2. Save the file as H.htm and open it in your browser.

Explanation

In contrast to inline-level elements (em, strong, span, etc.), block-level elements (div, P, H, etc.) are part of the so-called *box model*. Within these boxes various properties can be defined. These include `border-width` (absolute in px, or thin, medium, thick), `border-style` (none, hidden, solid, double, groove, ridge, inset or outset), and `border-color`. Try:

```
<DIV style="width:80%; text-align:center; border-style:groove;
border-color:red; border-width:medium"> This Text is shown in
```

```
80% of the DIV This Text is shown in 80% of the DIV This Text is
shown in 80% of the DIV This Text is shown in 80% of the DIV
This Text is shown in 80% of the DIV </DIV>
```

SUMMARY OF CSS: LINKS

<LINK> can appear only in the <HEAD> of an HTML file. The syntax is:

```
<LINK REL="stylesheet" TYPE="MIMEtype" HREF="filename.css">
```

There can be multiple links in <HEAD> and <STYLE> blocks, or in inline code elsewhere in the document. Links can be relative:

```
<LINK HREF="../../styles/filename.css">
```

or absolute:

```
<LINK HREF="http://www.fbeedle.com/styles/filename.css">
```

Conflicts are resolved using the cascading rules described earlier.

CSS2 defines *at-links*, which are implemented in MSIE 4, but not in Netscape 4. The syntax is:

```
<STYLE TYPE="MIMEtype">
@import url(filename.css)
</STYLE>
```

SUMMARY OF CSS: SELECTORS

There are three types of selectors:

- Class
- ID
- Contextual

Normal style rules could be, for example:

```
H1, H2 {color: red; text-transform: capitalize}
.....
<H1>capitals and red wherever H1 occurs in the document</H1>
```

(notice the concatenation syntax). *Class selectors* use `Class` to selectively specify where the rule should apply:

```
H1.title {color: red; text-transform: capitalize}
.title {color: red; text-transform: capitalize}
```

means:

```
<H1 Class="title">capitals and red because it is H1 and
class title</H1>
<H1>a header without capitals and red</H1>
<P Class="title">paragraph in capitals and red, because .title
applies to all elements of this class</p>
<P>normal paragraph because neither of the rules apply</p>
```

So `.title` applies to all elements declaring that `Class`, but it can also be made much more specific, using for example `H1.title`.

Contextual selectors build on Class selectors and are more specific. Perhaps you want a document consisting mostly of normal text (P, H1, H2, H3, etc.) where an effect is applied to italics. However, in some special headers the italics should have a different effect:

```
H2 {font-size: 18pt}
EM {font-weight: bold}
```

This will not do the job alone. A special EM has to be specified which takes effect only in the context of H2, thus

```
H2 EM {background-color: yellow}
```

is the Contextual selector specifying the effect applied to those EM elements which appear in the context of H2, but not in H1, H3, P, etc.

In contrast to Class and Context selectors, *ID selectors* must define a unique element in the document. The syntax does not use the dot (.) character, but rather uses the pound (#) character (also called a "hash" character).

```
#title {color: red; text-transform: capitalize}
```

means:

```
<DIV>is normal, but</DIV>
<DIV ID=title>is capitals and red</DIV>
<DIV ID=other>follows the rules for #other</DIV>
```

ID can be specified for any element, e.g., H1, H2, and P, as described above.

SUMMARY OF CSS: PSEUDO-CLASSES

A pseudo-class is in an interactive element that does not need to be defined with a Class selector. Presently, only the anchor tag (A) is a pseudo-class. A <STYLE> example could be:

```
<style type = "text/css">
a {text-decoration: none}
a: link {font-color: navy}
a: active {font-color: red}
a: visited {font-size: -1}
a: hover {text-decoration: underline}
</style>
```

JAVASCRIPT

HTML is read and interpreted in a passive fashion by a browser program. This is in contrast to JavaScript, which (like a program) is read and understood by a computer in an active and quite different fashion.

JavaScript is sometimes called a "scripting language," as if that were something simpler than a programming language. The exercises in this book will explore some of JavaScript's easier aspects, as JavaScript does have a number of features making it easier for the non-programmer. However, as the next paragraphs demonstrate, JavaScript is actually a full programming language, and certainly more complicated than several other programming languages!

Today, Netscape's JavaScript 1.1 (or its derivatives like Microsoft's JScript) are the *de facto* standards in Client-Side scripting; that is, they are coding "snippets," which are active when the computer involved is the individual's own PC (client). However, JavaScript is much more. It is also a powerful tool on the computer that hosts the web site (the server; server-side scripting). Many other applications, like Microsoft's "Active Server Pages," can be run using JavaScript (see my book, *ASP: Learning by Example*). It is worth noting that JavaScript can run server-side as well as client-side (as in DHTML).

Server-side and client-side JavaScript share the same core language. This core language corresponds to ECMA-262, the scripting language standardized by the European standards body (ECMA, European Computer Manufacturers Association), with some additions. The core language contains a set of core objects, such as the Array and Date objects. It also defines other language features such as its expressions, statements, and operators. Although server-side and client-side JavaScript use the same core functionality, in some cases they use them differently. In contrast to standard Common Gateway Interface (CGI) and Perl programs, all JavaScript is integrated directly into HTML pages. This means rapid development and easy maintenance. JavaScript's Session Management Service contains objects you can use to maintain data that persist across client requests, multiple clients, and multiple applications, like Structured Query Language (SQL).

On the server, JavaScript is also embedded in HTML pages. The server-side statements can connect to relational databases from different sources, share information across applications users, access the file system on the server, or communicate with other applications through, for example, Java. A compiled JavaScript application can also include client-side JavaScript in addition to server-side JavaScript.

In contrast to pure client-side JavaScript scripts, JavaScript applications that use server-side JavaScript are compiled into byte-code executable files. These application executables are run in concert with a web server that contains the JavaScript runtime engine (like Netscape Enterprise Server). For this reason, creating JavaScript applications is a two-stage process. In the first stage the developer creates HTML pages (which can contain both client-side and server-side JavaScript statements) and JavaScript files, which are then compiled into a single execut-able file. In the second stage, the application is requested by a client browser. The runtime engine uses the application executable to look up the source page and dynamically generate the HTML page to return. It runs any server-side JavaScript statements found on the page. The result of those statements might add new HTML or client-side JavaScript statements to the HTML page. The resulting page is then sent to the client browser, which displays the results.

CLIENT-SIDE JAVASCRIPT

Client-side JavaScript encompasses the core language plus extras such as the predefined objects, which are only relevant to running JavaScript in a browser. Server-side JavaScript encompasses the same core language plus extras such as the predefined objects and functions, which are only relevant to running JavaScript on a server. Servers-side JavaScript is beyond the scope of this book.

Client-side JavaScript is embedded directly in HTML pages and is interpreted by the browser upon running. Web browsers starting with Netscape Navigator 2.0 (and later versions) and Microsoft Internet Explorer 3.0 (and later versions) can inter-pret client-side JavaScript statements embedded in an HTML page (albeit that these very early browser versions only support the now-rare 1.0 version of JavaScript). When the browser (or client) requests such a page, the server sends the full content of the document, including HTML and JavaScript state-ments, over the Internet or other network (e.g., intranet) to the client. The client reads the page from top to bottom, displaying the results of the HTML and executing JavaScript statements as it goes. This process produces the results that the user sees.

Client-side JavaScript statements embedded in an HTML page can respond to user events such as mouse clicks, form input, and page navigation. For example, you can write a JavaScript function to verify that users enter valid information into a form requesting a telephone number or zip code. Without any network transmission, the embedded JavaScript on the HTML page can check the entered data and display a dialog box to the user who enters invalid data.

COMMENTS IN JAVASCRIPT

In HTML, commenting out lines uses:

```
<!--
here are several lines
of comments
-->
```

In JavaScript, double slash (//) is used to comment out a single line:

```
this is JavaScript code
// this line of code or comments is commented out
this is JavaScript code again
```

Many lines of code can be commented out using:

```
this is JavaScript code
/*
these lines of code
or comments are
commented out
*/
this is JavaScript code again
```

In order to hide JavaScript from older browsers and search engine robots, it is recommended to use the HTML and JavaScript methods in combination:

```
<script language="JavaScript>
<!-- // the above line has to be "seen" in HTML
// but neither HTML nor JavaScript should see this line
JavaScript code
/* comments
comments
comments */
more JavaScript code
// hide the "ending HTML comments" code from JavaScript -->
</script>
```

Note: Hiding the -- > from JavaScript is done using // -->, because using -- > alone will otherwise cause an error.

JAVASCRIPT OBJECTS

JavaScript has predefined objects for the core language, as well as additions for client-side and server-side JavaScript.

As described before in connection with HTML 4, objects have properties. Some properties can also be objects (e.g., by occurring as property values, so objects can appear to have sub-objects). What an object does is called a *method.* Some methods can be objects too.

Core objects include:

`Array, Boolean, Date, Function, Math, Number, Object, String.`
Some additional client-side objects include:

`Anchor, Applet, Area, Button, Checkbox, document, event, FileUpload, Form, Frame, Hidden, History, Image, Layer, Link, Location, MimeType, navigator, Option, Password, Plugin, Radio, Reset, screen, Select, Submit, Text, Textarea, Window`

These objects represent information relevant to working with JavaScript in a web browser. Objects can be put into *collections*. The *operator* used to connect them is a full stop (.). For example:

```
Form.element.radio.click
document.tags.body.color="red";
```

As noted above, many of these objects are related to each other by occurring as property values. For example, to access the images in a document, you use the document.images array, each of whose elements is an Image object.

Further details are given in Appendix B.

JAVASCRIPT STATEMENTS AND VARIABLES

Simple command lines are called *statements* or *expressions*. They are terminated by a semicolon (;). Semicolons separate statements; however, a new line will be interpreted by JavaScript as a semicolon. Thus:

```
return true;
```

is correct, but

```
return
true;
```

will be read as:

```
return; true
```

and thus will not work. So remember to open your ASCII editor and turn off the "automatic line break" functionality because it can ruin your work! If you have difficulty with the examples presented here, download the codes from the publisher's web site and compare them with what you have written.

Identifiers are the names used in *variables* and *functions*. Identifiers are case sensitive, and thus:

```
online
Online
OnLine
ONLINE
```

are four different names. The first character of an identifier has to be an ASCII letter; however, an underscore (_) or dollar ($) character is also acceptable. Numbers can be included in an identifier, but, as said, never in the first position. Avoid words like Script, language, HTML, as well as HTML tag, or DOM names (like bgColor). If you have trouble with your script then change the identifier, as it can often be a source of problems.

More Reserved Words

abstract	finally	reset
boolean	float	return
break	for	select
by	function	short
byte	goto	static
case	if	super
catch	implements	switch
char	import	synchronized
class	in	then
const	instanceof	this
continue	int	throw
default	interface	throws
delete	long	transient
dim	native	true
do	new	try
double	null	typeof
else	package	var
extends	private	void
false	protected	while
final	public	with

It is also an obviously unwise choice to name your variables method, property, attribute, subroutine, procedure, etc., because of the resulting confusion between, for example, a method and a variable called method.

VARIABLE TYPES

Variables are either declared or undeclared. *Declared variables* keep their value. Because they are permanent, this method is mostly used to declare *global variables*, whereas *local variables* remain undeclared. Variables are declared using `var`:

```
var i;
i = 2;
sum = i + 4;
```

Here the variable `i` is declared and set to 2 and will continue at this value. Notice that the equals sign (=) is not an arithmetic solution, but merely an assignment of content value. Note also that null is an empty value (void), and that zero (0) has a value; or to put it differently, the first 10 values are 0 to 9. Thus, for example, to check for non-occurrence, one has to check if the occurrence is minus one (-1) or null.

The variable `sum` is not declared. Above, it assumes the value 6, but this may change later. JavaScript variables are untyped, that is, they may contain different types of data.

```
i = 2
i = A
i = "Hello"
```

are all perfectly acceptable. In the first case, the variable contains an integer, so multiplication, addition, and other operations can be performed. In the second case, the variable contains a single letter (which may be a variable and thus contain an integer). In the third case, the variable contains a *string literal* (indicated by the quotation marks). Clearly, multiplication, addition, etc. cannot be performed on strings, but concatenation (always denoted by a plus (+) sign) can:

Addition of Numbers	Addition (Concatenation) of Strings
A=1	variable1="A"
B=2	variable2="B"
A+B=3	variable1 + variable2 = AB

JavaScript has a characteristic that is very beginner-friendly; it will convert variable types as appropriate:

```
Z = "55"
Y = Z+1
```

So even though Z is originally defined as being a string, it will be automatically converted to an integer so that 1 can be added to it, so Y = 56.

String literals are character sequences that are written literally to the screen. String literals include spacebar characters.

Obviously, quotation marks and some other characters can cause problems. There are two ways around this. Thankfully, mixing single (') and double (") quotation marks is not usually a problem in JavaScript;

```
"this is something 'and this is something else' "
'this is something "and this is something else" '
```

are normally interchangeable, provided they are not part of a larger string. *Escape sequences* can also be used. Escaping a tag with a trailing slash (/) sign was noted earlier in connection with XHTML. However, in JavaScript, escaping is accomplished using a backslash (\) immediately preceding the character to be escaped:

```
"ignore the \" quotation mark"
document.write("<\/script>");
```
—useful if you are dynamically writing scripts

Yet some escape sequences are reserved: \n donates a new line, \t donates a tab stop, \f is a form feed, \b is a backspace, and \r is a carriage return.

JAVASCRIPT FUNCTIONS

Functions can be declared or anonymous. *Declared functions* assume the style function *name(argument)*. For example:

```
function square(x)
{
return x*x;
}
```

However, *anonymous functions* can easily give the same result:

```
var square = function(x) {return x*x;}
```

Note the use of curly braces ({}) to hold a collection of statements as well as the use of the multiplication (*) operator. Functions are called using the function name and brackets, e.g.:

```
square()
```

where the brackets may, if needed, contain an *argument*. For example:

```
alert("Welcome")
```

where the string literal "Welcome" is the argument. There are also a number of standard functions; the most useful will be presented in their context during the examples.

JAVASCRIPT OPERATORS

Operators for multiplication of numbers and concatenation of strings have already been presented. The following is a non-exhaustive list of the most useful operators. L or R in the left-hand column denotes whether the associativity is L (left-to-right) or R (right-to-left). These operators are examined and explained more thoroughly in the examples.

Associativity	Operator	Operand Type	Operation Performed
L	.	object property	access to properties
L	[ ]	array, integer	array index
L	( )	function arguments	function call
R	new	constructor call	create new object
L	*	numbers	multiplication
L	/	numbers	division
L	%	numbers	remainder (modulo)
L	+	numbers	addition
L	+	strings	concatenation
L	–	numbers	subtraction
R	++	numbers	pre- or post increment (stepwise of 1)
R	--	numbers	pre- or post decrement (stepwise of 1)
R	!	boolean	logical complement
R	typeof	any	return data type
L	<	numbers or strings	less than
L	<=	numbers or strings	less than or equal to
L	>	numbers or strings	greater than
L	>=	numbers or strings	greater than or equal to

R	=	any variable	assignment
L	==	any	test for equality
L	===	any	test for exact identity
L	!=	any	test for inequality
L	!==	any	test for non-identity
L	&	integers	and
L	|	integers	or
L	&&	boolean	logical and
L	||	boolean	logical or
L	,	any	multiple evaluation

JAVASCRIPT CONDITIONAL STATEMENTS

The most common conditional statement is "If" (or "If/Else," or "If/Else-If/Else").
See if you can understand the functions, statements, escaped characters, and operators in the following three illustrations:

```
1. if (username==null) username="guest";
2. if ((username==null) || (username==""))
{
username="undefined";
alert("please submit a user name");
}
3. if (username !=null)
alert("Hello " + username + "\nWelcome");
else
{
```

```
username=prompt("Welcome\nwhat is your name");
alert("Hello, " + username);
}
```

Clearly, `if` is a test (or *condition*), and `else` is a catch-all alternative. However, a series of tests can also be accomplished by using `else if`. In the following illustration code 1 is to be performed if the variable n has a value of 1, code 2 if n's value is 2, and so on. Finally, if n's value is more than 3, then a "catch all" is invoked:

```
if (n==1) {code1;}
else if (n==2) {code2;}
else if (n==3) {code3;}
else {catch-all code;}
```

Notice here that one could also have said:

```
else if (n>3) {catch-all code;}
```

Example I: Calling JavaScript

In a similar fashion to what was explained regarding CSS, there are three ways of specifying JavaScript:

- Inline: Exactly where it is needed.

- Declared: In a <SCRIPT></SCRIPT> block, normally (but not always) in <HEAD>.

- External: In a separate file. Whereas external files in CSS have the extension .css, external files containing JavaScript code have the extension .js.

Whichever way you decide to write your JavaScript, it is a good idea to have the code as high up towards the beginning of the HTML document as possible so that the code has been read in before it should be performed.

1. Open your HTML or ASCII editor and type:

```
<HTML>
<HEAD>
</HEAD>
<BODY>
<P language=javascript
OnClick="alert('Welcome');">Click
here</P>
</BODY>
</HTML>
```

2. Save the file as I1.htm.

3. Open I1.htm in your browser and click on the text.

4. Open your HTML or ASCII editor and type:

```
<HTML>
<HEAD>
<script language="javascript">
function start()
{
alert("Welcome");
}
</script>
</HEAD>
<BODY>
<P OnClick="start()">Click here</P>
</BODY>
</HTML>
```

5. Save the file as I2.htm.

6. Open I2.htm in your browser and click on the text.

7. Open your HTML or ASCII editor and type:

```
function start()
{
alert("Welcome");
}
```

8. Save the file as I3.js.

9. Open your HTML or ASCII editor and type:

```
<HTML>
<HEAD>
<SCRIPT TYPE="text/javascript"
LANGUAGE="JavaScript" SRC="I3.js">
</SCRIPT>
</HEAD>
<BODY>
<P OnClick="start()">Click here</P>
</BODY>
</HTML>
```

10. Save the file as I3.htm.

11. Open I3.htm in your browser and click on the text.

Explanation

The functionality in the files I1.htm, I2.htm and I3.htm is similar. In all three there is one paragraph of text connected with an *event handler* (OnClick). OnClick invokes an Alert box of the general form:

```
alert()
```

which contains an argument, in these cases a string literal "Welcome". In I1.htm the Alert box is invoked directly using inline code. In both I2.htm and I3.htm the function start is invoked:

```
OnClick="start()"
```

where the function is defined either in the HEAD of the same HTML document (as in I2.htm) or, in I3.htm, in an external file (I3.js). In both I2.htm and I3.htm the code is contained within <SCRIPT> </SCRIPT> blocks. However, in I3.htm only the MIME type and URL (SRC=) of the code file are given, while all the code is written in I3.js.

Example J builds on Example I to illustrate the Microsoft DOM.

Example J: Object Model and Collections

In the DHTML Object Model (DOM), everything in a web document (elements, forms, frames, tables, etc.) is seen as an object. The programmer can give these objects attributes either by using ALL (everything, in the order they are defined in the document) or by giving objects an appropriate identity.

1. Open your HTML or ASCII editor and type:

```
<HTML>
<HEAD>
<script language="javascript">
function start()
{alert(pText.innerText);
```

```
pText.innerText="Welcome";}
</script>
</head>
<body onLoad="start()">
<P ID="pText">click OK and come on in</P>
</body>
</HTML>
```

2. Save the file as J.htm and open it in your browser.

Explanation

A JavaScript function called start() is defined. This is called as the BODY loads (<Body OnLoad="start()">). This function takes the inner text from the element with the identity (ID) pText and shows it in an Alert Box. Notice that pText is in a P element in BODY. After clicking OK, the content of the variable pText is redefined (="Welcome") in HEAD, and that is shown in the BODY instead of the original pText.

Note that Netscape Navigator will not accept innerText, as it is not in Netscape's DOM.

Examples I and J have introduced two event handlers. Before more JavaScript is introduced, here is a list of common event handlers and their applicability to the Microsoft and Netscape DOMs. Most of the event handlers' functions can be understood from their names, and therefore it is not hard to understand what the following codes will do:

```
<BODY onLoad="alert('Hello and welcome');"
onUnload="alert('Goodbye, see you again soon');">
```

or:

```
<FORM>
<INPUT TYPE="BUTTON" onClick="document.bgColor='yellow';" VALUE="Click for yellow
background">
<P>
<INPUT TYPE="BUTTON" onMouseDown="document.bgColor='red';" VALUE="Press for red
background">
<P>
<INPUT TYPE="BUTTON" onMouseUp="window.status='Blue
background';document.bgColor='blue'" VALUE="Press and let go for blue background">
<P>
<INPUT TYPE="BUTTON" onMouseOver="window.status='Black
background';document.bgColor='black';" VALUE="Roll the mouse over for black
background">
<P>
<INPUT TYPE="BUTTON" onMouseOut="window.status='Green
background';document.bgColor='green';" VALUE="Roll the mouse off for green
background">
</FORM>
```

AN OVERVIEW OF EVENT HANDLERS

Useful, effective in both Netscape 4+ and MSIE 4+		Less used, but still effective in both Netscape 4+ and MSIE 4+		
Onblur	Onload	Onabort	Onkeypress	Onmouseup
Onclick	Onreset	Ondblclick	Onkeyup	Onreset
Onfocus	Onsubmit	Onerror	Onmousedown	Onresize
Onmouseout	Onunload	Onkeydown	Onmousemove	
Onmouseover	Onselect			

Used infrequently, mostly effective only in MSIE 4+		
Onafterupdate	Onafterprint	Ondrag
Onbeforeupdate	Onbeforecopy	Ondragend
Ondataavailable	Onbeforecut	Ondragenter
Ondatasetchange	Onbeforeeditfocus	Ondragleave
Ondatasetcomplete	Onbeforepaste	Ondragover
Onerrorupdate	Onbeforeprint	Ondragstart
Onhelp	Onbeforeunload	Ondrop
Onreadystatechange	Onbeforeupdate	Onfinish
Onrowenter	Onbounce	Onpaste
Onrowexit	Oncellchange	Onpropertychange
Ondragstart	Onchange	Onrowinserted
Onfilterchange	Oncontextmenu	Onscroll
Onhelp	Oncopy	Onstart
Onselectstart	Oncut	Onstop

Example K: Variables and Methods

1. Open your HTML or ASCII editor and type:

```
<HTML>
<HEAD>
<TITLE>Variables and methods</TITLE>
</HEAD>
<BODY>
```

```
<SCRIPT LANGUAGE="JAVASCRIPT">
<!--
    name = "Rob Mellor";
    age = 47
    document.write("Author of this book: " + name);
    document.write(". On the 19th of November 2002 he is: " + age);
// -->
</SCRIPT>
</BODY>
</HTML>
```

2. Save the file as K1.htm and open it in your browser.

3. Open your HTML or ASCII editor and type:

```
<HTML>
<HEAD>
<TITLE>Variables and methods 2</TITLE>
</HEAD>
<BODY>
<SCRIPT LANGUAGE="JAVASCRIPT">
<!--
name = "Rob Mellor";
age = 47
document.write("The author of this book is called: " + name.bold());
document.write("<P>On the 19th of November 2002 he is: " + age);
document.write("<P>His full name is:<P>" + "Dr. " + name.bold().fontsize(6));
// -->
</SCRIPT>
</BODY>
</HTML>
```

4. Save the file as K2.htm and open it in your browser.

Explanation

In K1.htm two local variables were declared and assigned values (one a string literal, the other an integer). The document object's method called `write` was then accessed using dot syntax. This method then (twice) wrote a string literal concatenated with a variable. Note that the variable is simply called using its name, but its content is written to the screen. Clearly, the write method could have been accessed once and the whole message printed out at once:

```
document.write("Author of this book: " + name + ". On the 19th
of November 2002 he is: " + age);
```

K2.htm followed exactly the same pattern, with the exception that the variable name has two methods (`bold` and `fontsize`), which were accessed using dot syntax and printed in a third line. Notice especially that the string literals can contain HTML code (in this case <P>), which is interpreted as HTML and thus helps with the layout on dynamic pages.

Example L: Functions and Parameters

1. Open your HTML or ASCII editor and type:

```
<HTML>
<HEAD>
<TITLE>Calling a simple function</TITLE>
<SCRIPT LANGUAGE="JAVASCRIPT">
function greeting()
{
document.write("<HR>Hello world<HR>");
}
</SCRIPT>
</HEAD>
```

```
<BODY>
<SCRIPT LANGUAGE="JAVASCRIPT">
  greeting();
  greeting();
</SCRIPT>
</BODY>
</HTML>
```

2. Save the file as L1.htm and open it in your browser.

3. Open your HTML or ASCII editor and type:

```
<HTML>
<HEAD>
<TITLE>function with parameter</TITLE>
<SCRIPT LANGUAGE="JAVASCRIPT">
function test(mytext)
{
document.write("<FONT SIZE=7>" + mytext + "</FONT>");
}
</SCRIPT>
</HEAD>
<BODY>
<SCRIPT LANGUAGE="JAVASCRIPT">
test("very large text");
</SCRIPT>
</BODY>
</HTML>
```

4. Save the file as L2.htm and open it in your browser.

5. Open your HTML or ASCII editor and type:

```
<HTML>
<HEAD>
<TITLE>a function with 2 parameters</TITLE>
<SCRIPT LANGUAGE="JAVASCRIPT">
function test(mytext, textbig)
{
document.write("<FONT SIZE=" + textbig + ">" + mytext + "</FONT><BR>");
}
</SCRIPT>
</HEAD>
<BODY>

<SCRIPT LANGUAGE="JAVASCRIPT">
    test("large text", 5);
    test("larger text", 6);
    test("largest text", 7);
</SCRIPT>

</BODY>
</HTML>
```

6. Save the file as L3.htm and open it in your browser.

7. Open your HTML or ASCII editor and type:

```
<HTML>
<HEAD>
<TITLE>calling a function with parameters and calculation</TITLE>
<SCRIPT LANGUAGE="JAVASCRIPT">
movedown = "<p>";
function plus(a,b)
{
```

```
return theresult = a+b
}
</SCRIPT>
</HEAD>
<BODY>
<SCRIPT LANGUAGE="JAVASCRIPT">
test = plus(2,8);
// here is a variable as a function
document.write("2 plus 8 equals: ",test + movedown);
document.write("12 plus 43 equals: ",plus(12,43));
</SCRIPT>
</BODY>
</HTML>
```

8. Save the file as L4.htm and open it in your browser.

Explanation

L1.htm is a repeat demonstration of the simple function, using `document.write` to print an HTML-containing string literal. L1.htm further demonstrates that <SCRIPT> blocks can easily be defined in <BODY> and can be called several times.

In the <BODY> of L2.htm the function test is called, with a string literal as argument:

```
test("very large text");
```

This is simply placed in the parameter (`mytext`) as defined in the function code (in <HEAD>), which in turn is printed to the screen exactly as a variable is and concatenated with HTML code using a plus sign (+):

```
document.write("<FONT SIZE=7>" + mytext + "</FONT>");
```

In L3.htm there are two parameters, joined with the comma (,) operator for multiple evaluation. Notice now that the font size has become a variable and how that is written dynamically to the page:

```
"<FONT SIZE=" + textbig + ">"
```

In L4.htm a local variable (movedown) is made, which simply holds the HTML. The variable (test) is made, which defines the input to the function plus. These can then be printed to the screen:

```
"2 plus 8 equals: ",test + movedown);
```

Notice the text string, then the comma (,) operator for multiple evaluation, and then the concatenation with the variable (movedown). The second line of writing inputs directly into the function:

```
plus(12,43)
```

which simply gives the input to the function named plus:

```
function plus(a,b)
{
    return theresult = a+b
}
```

This illustrates that there are several ways of calculating and writing the result to the screen. Until now these examples have been "hardwired," with the primary data already written into the HTML file. However, Example M can calculate new data.

Example M: Conditional Statements and Loops

1. Open your ASCII or HTML editor and type:

```
<TITLE>simple loop with condition</TITLE>
</HEAD>
<BODY>
```

```
<SCRIPT LANGUAGE="JAVASCRIPT">
for (i=1;i<21;i++)
document.write(i + " ");
document.write("<p>or if you do not like 13:<p>");
for (i=1;i<21;i++)
if (i != 13)
document.write(i + " ");
</SCRIPT>
</BODY>
</HTML>
```

2. Save the document as M1.htm.

3. Open M1.htm in your browser.

4. Open your ASCII or HTML editor and type:

```
<HTML>
<HEAD>
<TITLE>Loop with condition and confirm</TITLE>
</HEAD>
<BODY>
<SCRIPT LANGUAGE="JAVASCRIPT">
if (confirm("are you superstitious?"))
{
for (i=1;i<21;i++)
if (i != 13) document.write(i + " ");
}
else
{
for (i=1;i<21;i++)
document.write(i + " ");
}
```

```
</SCRIPT>
</BODY>
</HTML>
```

5. Save the document as M2.htm.

6. Open M2.htm in your browser.

7. Open your ASCII or HTML editor and type:

```
<HTML>
<HEAD>
</HEAD>
<BODY>
<h1>Change Color</h1>
<SCRIPT LANGUAGE="JAVASCRIPT">
textcolor = 256
for (color=1;color<256;color++)
{
textcolor--
document.bgColor=65536*color+256*color+color;
document.fgColor=65536*textcolor+256*textcolor+textcolor;
}
//note that fgColor does not work in Netscape!
</SCRIPT>
</BODY>
</HTML>
```

8. Save the document as M3.htm.

9. Open M3.htm in your browser, and refresh the browser several times.

Explanation

Example M sets up a loop (`for`) specifying a variable (`i`). That variable is set to have a value of 1:

```
for (i=1
```

Using the multiple evaluator semicolon (`;`), the next expression specifies that the highest value which `i` can reach is less than 21 (i.e., is 20):

```
for (i=1;i<21
```

Using semicolon again, we specify that for each loop the value of `i` is incremented by 1:

```
for (i=1;i<21;i++)
```

And for each loop, the value which `i` has reached is printed to the screen:

```
document.write(i + " ");
```

where the concatenation `+ " ");` simply adds a white space (space bar) for cosmetic reasons.

In the second for-loop a condition is added, such that the above mechanism only works when `i` is not 13:

```
if (i != 13)
```

Of course, `i` reached 13 (because it also reached 14 and subsequent numbers), but the condition prevents `document.write` from taking effect when `i` = 13.

M2.htm is very similar to M1.htm. Here a Confirm Box (similar to the Alert Box demonstrated earlier, but with two buttons) is opened:

```
if (confirm("are you superstitious?"))
```

and then, according to the results, either the first or the second for-loop is activated.

The principle behind M3.htm is the same. The two variables `textcolor` and `color` in principle refer to background and foreground colors (`bgColor` and `fgColor`, but we can't use them directly because they are reserved words). `textcolor` is set to 256 and decreased (decremented):

```
textcolor = 256
{
textcolor--
```

while `color` is set to 1 and incremented:

```
for (color=1;color<256;color++)
```

1. To continue this example, re-open your ASCII or HTML editor and type:

```
<HTML>
<HEAD>
</HEAD>
<BODY>
<SCRIPT LANGUAGE="JAVASCRIPT">
age = prompt("How old are you?","");
if (age <=18)
{
document.write("you are too young!");
document.bgColor="Black";
document.fgColor="White";
```

Type of Box	Syntax	Appearance
Alert	`alert(argument)`	Contains a statement (string literal) and only one button, "OK."
Confirm	`confirm(argument)`	Contains a statement (string literal) and two buttons, returning True or False.
Prompt	`prompt(argument),""`	Contains a statement and two buttons (OK and reset) together with an input box to put data into the system.

```
}
else if (age >- 80)
{
document.write("you are too old");
document.bgColor="#663366";
document.fgColor="#ff33ff";
}
else
document.write("Welcome");
</SCRIPT>
</BODY>
</HTML>
```

2. Save the document as M4.htm.

3. Open M4.htm in your browser.

4. Enter the value 10 in the prompt box, refresh the browser, and repeat with 50, 100, and other numbers.

Explanation

M4.htm illustrates the same principle again, only the Prompt Box is slightly different from the Alert Box and Confirm Box seen previously, and allows the client to input data. This data is then used in the `if` conditional selection.

Example N: Conditional Statements, Operators, and Standard Functions

Previously "hard-wired" or client-derived data has been used (as in Example M) to either define variable content, or to calculate from given starting points. In Example N, external data is used as a basis input.

1. Open your ASCII or HTML editor and type:

```
<HTML>
<HEAD>
```

```
</HEAD>
<BODY>
<SCRIPT LANGUAGE="JAVASCRIPT">
document.bgColor="White";
dato = new Date();
dayornight = dato.getDay();
if (dayornight == 1)
{
document.bgColor="Black";
document.fgColor="White";
document.write ("Black Monday");
}
if (dayornight >= 1 && dayornight < 5)
document.write("The rest of the week, days two to four");
if (dayornight >= 5 || dayornight < 1)
document.write("But weekends are best");
</SCRIPT>
</BODY>
</HTML>
```

2. Save the document as N1.htm.

3. Open N1.htm in your browser.

4. Change the day on your computer (double-click on the clock in the Start menu bar).

5. Refresh your browser; then repeat for other days.

Explanation

N1.htm uses the object's document and date together with their respective methods, write and getDay. A variable called dato uses the operator (and thus reserved word) new to create a new instance of the object date. A new variable (dayornight) contains the value of Dates method, getDay. getDay returns the day of the week in numerical form, so Monday is one, Tuesday two, Wednesday is three, and so forth. These can be tested using an if condition:

```
dato = new Date();
dayornight = dato.getDay();
if (dayornight == 1)
```

The remaining if conditions are purely mechanical. In this case they simply illustrate the use of the operators: =, ==, >=, >, >=, >, &&, and ||.

1. To continue this example, re-open your ASCII or HTML editor and type:

```
<HTML>
<head>
<script language="JavaScript">
rightnowday = new Date();
rightnowtime = rightnowday.getHours();
if (rightnowtime>6 && rightnowtime<20)
{
window.location.href="day.htm";
}
else
{
window.location.href="night.htm";
}
</script>
<title>Script forwarding the user dependent on the returned
time</title>
</head>
<body>
```

```
</body>
</HTML>
```

2. Save the document as N2.htm.

3. Make two new HTML documents, day.htm and night.htm, with distinctive `bgColors`.

4. Open N2.htm in your browser.

5. Reset the time in your computer (see above).

6. Refresh your browser, and then repeat.

Explanation

N2.htm is in principle the same as N1.htm, just that now instead of

`getDay()`

the method

`getHours()`

is used, which simply returns the hours as a numerical value of the 24-hour clock. Depending (using the `if` condition) on the value returned, then the client is forwarded to either one of two files using:

`window.location.href="night.htm";`

but `document.location.href` (or `parent.location.href`, when using frames) could also have been used. However, using `window` has the advantage that you can easily go backward and forward using `window`'s `history` object:

```
<input type="button" value="< - back "
onClick="window.history.back();">
<input type="button" value="forwards - >"
onClick="window.history.forward();">
```

Home Exercise 1: Forms and Arrays, a 24 hour On-Line Pizza Bar

You have a customer who has requested that you make a small web site for him and his pizza bar. His experience is that customers are willing to pay more for the same pizza if it is nighttime, so there should be a price differential. Customers must be able to order pizzas directly over the Internet However, since this is only an exercise, the FORM element should not actually send an order, so use INPUT TYPE="BUTTON" instead of SUBMIT. This should return an Alert Box stating that the pizza is ready in 20 minutes.

Your web site should contain an index that is light colored, between 07.00 and 20.00, but otherwise uses dark colors (this can either be in index, or index can send the client to the appropriate file). Nighttime prices are 75% higher than day-time prices. The price list is shown in a JavaScript array (sample code below, and see Example O). The table is contained in a FORM element, where clients can check one or more checkboxes of their choice (written dynamically using JavaScript). A suggestion to the array code is:

```
<HTML>
<head>
<script language="JavaScript">
document.bgColor="#FFFFFF";
document.fgColor="#000000";
warenr=1
// function writing the table rows
function writerows(ware,price)
{
document.write("<TR><TD><INPUT TYPE='CHECKBOX'></TD><TD>" + warenr + "</TD><TD>"
+ ware + "</TD><TD>$. " + price + "</TD></TR>");
// don't forget that is all on one line
warenr++;
}
</script>
</HEAD>
<BODY>
<H1>This is the 24 hour Pizza Bar</H1>
```

```
<form>
<table border="0">
<tr bgcolor="silver"><td>Order</td><td>Ware Number</td>
<td>Pizza</td><td>Price</td></tr>
<script language="JAVASCRIPT">
writerows ("pizza", 12);
writerows ("hot dog", 16);
writerows ("burger", 16);
writerows ("steak sandwich", 23);
writerows ("beer", 8);
writerows ("wine", 10);
</script>
<tr><td colspan=4 align="center"><input type="button"
value="Order here" onClick="alert('Thank you for your
order,\nYou can collect your order in 20 minutes')">
 <input type="reset" value="reset"></td></tr>
</table>
</form>
</font>
</HTML>
```

It will obviously be a bit awkward to multiply these prices up by 75% and enter in the new prices by hand, so the following modification in the script might be useful for the "night-side":

```
warenr=1
nightfee=1.75
function writerows (ware,price)
{
document.write("<TR><TD><INPUT TYPE='CHECKBOX'></TD><TD>"
+ warenr + "</TD><TD>" + ware + "</TD><TD>$. "
+ Math.ceil(price*nightfee) + "</TD></TR>");
```

```
warenr++;
}
```

Go to the library or use other reference works (including the web links at the end of this book) to look up Math functions like `Math.ceil`, `Math.floor`, and `Math.random`.

Example O: Arrays

Arrays are tables which, like a Recordset, are read into the PC's RAM and can be read from there somewhat like a database.

1. Open your ASCII or HTML editor and type:

```
<HTML>
<HEAD>
<TITLE>Array</TITLE>
<SCRIPT LANGUAGE = "JavaScript">
citation = new Array();
citation[0] = "do not use SCRIPT-tags with event handlers.";
citation[1] = "develop your web-site using Netscape 3 and a
15 inch screen."
citation[2] = "do not mix HTML3.2 and HTML4."
citation[3] = "remember that JavaScript is case-sensitive."
function anyOne(position)
{
whichOne = Math.floor(Math.random()*position);
return whichOne;
}
</SCRIPT>
</HEAD>
<BODY>
<SCRIPT LANGUAGE = "JavaScript">
```

```
document.write(citation[anyOne(citation.length)])
</SCRIPT>
</BODY>
</html>
```

2. Save the document as O.htm.

3. Open O.htm in your browser.

4. Refresh the browser several times.

Explanation

A new array is created and assigned to a variable called `citation`:

```
citation = new Array();
```

This array can be compared to a table consisting of only one column and four rows. The numbering of the rows follows the JavaScript convention that the first number is zero, and it is accessed using square brackets (`[]`):

```
citation[0] = "do not use SCRIPT-tags with event handlers.";
```

Although, as the sample code in Home Exercise 1 shows, either the index number or a string value can be used. To achieve more columns than the one-column example shown, concatenation with a comma (`,`) is used, for example:

```
myarray[0,0]
myarray[0,1]
```

Arrays are very useful in other respects. Because all the arrays components are loaded, it can be used to "pre-load," for example, image files which then can be used by event handlers like mouse-overs to very rapidly show the effect. See Example Y for more details.

Example P: Environmental Variables and Browser Check

Environmental variables are a kind of "handshake" a browser uses when requesting information like a file. These can easily be used to make choices based on if conditions. The Navigator object represents the browser application itself. It has five properties, two collections, and two methods:

Properties	Description
appCodeName	The browser's code name
appName	The browser's product name
appVersion	The browser's version number
cookieEnabled	If client-side cookies are accepted
userAgent	The user agent (browser name) header sent in HTTP

Collections	Description
mimeTypes	The types of files supported by that browser
plugins	An alias for the collection of all the <EMBED> objects in a page

Methods	Description
taintEnabled	A Netscape (only) method, returns false
javaEnabled	Indicates if the browser can execute Java code

1. Open your ASCII or HTML editor and type:

    ```
    <HTML>
    ```

```
<HEAD>
<TITLE>Browsercheck - simple</TITLE>
</HEAD>
<BODY>
<H2>
<SCRIPT LANGUAGE="JAVASCRIPT">
browser = navigator.appName;
ver = navigator.appVersion;
if (navigator.appName == "Netscape")
document.write("You are using Netscape - version ", ver);
else
document.write("You are using ",browser , ", version ", ver);
</SCRIPT>
</BODY>
</HTML>
```

2. Save the document as P1.htm.

3. Open P1.htm in your browser.

4. Open your ASCII or HTML editor and type:

```
<HTML>
<HEAD>
<TITLE>Browsercheck - advanced</TITLE>
</HEAD>
<BODY>
<H2>
<SCRIPT LANGUAGE="JAVASCRIPT">
browser = navigator.appName;
ver = navigator.appVersion;
monitor = screen.colorDepth;
browserplatform = navigator.platform
```

```
browcpu = navigator.cpuClass
browonline = navigator.onLine
document.write("color setup (bits): " + monitor + "<br>")
document.write("Platform: " + browserplatform + "<br>")
document.write("CPU: " + browcpu + "<br>")
document.write("Online: " + browonline + "<br>")
if (navigator.appName == "Netscape")
document.write("You are using Netscape - version ", ver);
else
document.write("You are using ",browser , " i version ", ver);
</SCRIPT>
</H2>
</BODY>
</HTML>
```

5. Save the document as P2.htm.

6. Open P2.htm in your browser.

7. Open your ASCII or HTML editor and type:

```
<HTML>
<HEAD>
<TITLE>Browsercheck - redirect</TITLE>
</HEAD>
<BODY>
<SCRIPT LANGUAGE="JAVASCRIPT">
browser = navigator.appName;
if (browser == "Netscape")
{
window.location.href="http://www.netscape.com"
}
else if (browser == "Microsoft Internet Explorer")
```

```
{
window.location.href="http://www.microsoft.com"
}
else
{
alert("Hey, what browser are you using ?");
}
</SCRIPT>
</BODY>
</HTML>
```

8. Save the document as P3.htm.

9. Open P3.htm in your browser.

Explanation for the Fourth Part

In the next part of the example, we will need six different files. P4.htm is a frameset document with two frames, called `navigation` and `main`. In main we load a document called P5.htm, which contains our code. We also need four empty HTML files with different background colors.

1. To continue this example, re-open your ASCII or HTML editor and type:

```
<html>
<head>
</head>
<frameset cols="20%,*">
<frame name="navigation" src="yellow.htm">
<frame name="main" src="P5.htm">
</frameset>
</html>
```

2. Save the document as P4.htm.

3. Open a new document and type:

```
<HTML>
<HEAD>
<script language="javascript">
<!--
function check()
{if (navigator.appName == "Microsoft Internet Explorer" &&
navigator.appVersion >= "4.0")
{parent.navigation.location="red.htm"}
else if (navigator.appName == "Netscape" &&
navigator.appVersion >= "4.0")
{parent.navigation.location="green.htm"}
else {parent.navigation.location="blue.htm"}
}
// -->
</script>
</head>
<body bgcolor="#FFFFFF" OnLoad="check()">
<P>here is main</p>
</body>
</html>
```

4. Save the document as P5.htm. Open a new document and type:

```
<HTML><HEAD></HEAD><BODY bgcolor="yellow"></BODY></HTML>
```

5. Save the document as yellow.htm. Open a new document and type:

```
<HTML><HEAD></HEAD><BODY bgcolor="red"></BODY></HTML>
```

6. Save the document as red.htm. Open a new document and type:

```
<HTML><HEAD></HEAD><BODY bgcolor="blue"></BODY></HTML>
```

7. Save the document as blue.htm. Open a new document and type:

```
<HTML><HEAD></HEAD><BODY bgcolor="green"></BODY></HTML>
```

8. Save the document as green.htm.

9. Open P4.htm in various browsers (Netscape 3, Netscape 4, Explorer 4, etc.).

Explanation

In the simple browser check illustrated in P1.htm, two methods (appName and appVersion) of the object navigator are used.

```
navigator.appName;
ver = navigator.appVersion;
if (navigator.appName == "Netscape")
```

Notice the exact equality sign (==). This is needed because some browsers, like MSIE, will introduce itself as both Explorer and as Netscape. The point is to tell the server, "I am actually Explorer, but I can do what Netscape can do."

If appName is exactly equal to Netscape, then a choice is made:

```
document.write("You are using Netscape - version ", ver);
```

where the content of the variable ver is printed to the screen.

The script in P2.htm simply builds on this, using more methods of the navigator object: platform, cpuClass, and onLine:

```
browserplatform = navigator.platform
browcpu = navigator.cpuClass
browonline = navigator.onLine
```

as well as introducing the screen object and its method, colorDepth:

```
monitor = screen.colorDepth;
```

P3.htm is simply a variation on the theme, introducing redirect (`window.location`, as seen before) and an Alert Box possibility.

P5.htm is called into P4.htm as soon as this is opened. Upon P5.htm BODY being loaded, the function `check()` is called. This is one of the major reasons why <SCRIPT> blocks are normally written in <HEAD>; they are not shown in the browser, and they are already loaded before they are called.

The function `check()` uses:

```
navigator.appName
```

to find out which browser is used, and

```
navigator.appVersion
```

to find out which version number it is. These data are then used in a simple if-else statement according to whether the Agent is Netscape 4+, or Explorer 4+, or ELSE (all others). Notice the Boolean operators `&&`, making it possible to combine `appName` and `appVersion`. According to which of the three possibilities are fulfilled, `parent.navigation.location` is set to which file should be shown in the left side of the frames document, e.g., `="blue.htm"`.

As mentioned in Example N, JavaScript will find the largest object available. In Example N it was the HTML file (called `document` or `window` in JavaScript). Here, however, the largest object is not document (which is only P5.htm), but is the frame's document (P4.htm). The part of this we are interested in is called navigation, so it is easy to set the frame's property location to be a different colored file according to browser and version.

Example Q: Setting Cookies with JavaScript

Cookies are part of the personalization of the Internet. They allow returning clients not to be bothered by things they have seen before, see your web site in the color they prefer, etc.

1. Open your ASCII or HTML editor and type:

```
<HTML>
<HEAD>
<SCRIPT LANGUAGE= "JavaScript">
<!--
// this function collects a cookie.
function getthatCookie(name){
var cname = name + "=";
var dc = document.cookie;
if (dc.length > 0) {
getgoing = dc.indexOf(cname);
if (getgoing != -1) {
getgoing += cname.length;
endit = dc.indexOf(";", getgoing);
```

```
if (endit == -1) endit = dc.length;
return unescape(dc.substring(getgoing, endit));
}
}
return null;
}
// this function saves a cookie
function savethatCookie(name, value, until) {
document.cookie = name + "=" + escape(value) + "; path=/" +
((until == null) ? "" : "; expires=" + until.toGMTString());
}
// this function deletes a cookie
function getridofCookie(name) {
document.cookie = name + "=; expires=Thu,
01-Jan-70 00:00:01 GMT" +  "; path=/";
}
var udl = new Date();
udl.setTime(udl.getTime() +  (24 * 60 * 60 * 1000 * 365));
amount=getthatCookie("visit");
// -->
</SCRIPT>
<title>Cookies - Visit counter</title>
</HEAD>
<BODY BGCOLOR = "#FFFFFF">
<SCRIPT LANGUAGE="JavaScript">
if (amount==null){
document.write("Welcome, this is your first visit.");
amount+=2;
savethatCookie("visit",amount,udl);
}
else {
```

```
document.write("Hi again, this is your visit number " +
getthatCookie("visit") + " to this site.");
amount++;
savethatCookie("visit",amount,ud1);
}
</SCRIPT>
<P><A HREF="#" onClick="getridofCookie('visit')">Click here
to delete the cookie and reset.</A>
</BODY>
</HTML>
```

2. Save the document as Q1.htm.

3. Open Q1.htm in your browser.

   This kind of script can easily be transferred to an external file.

4. Open your ASCII or HTML editor and type:

```
var ud1 = new Date();
ud1.setTime(ud1.getTime() + (24 * 60 * 60 * 1000 * 365));
// this function collect the cookie.
function getthatCookie(name){
var cname = name + "=";
var dc = document.cookie;
if (dc.length > 0) {
getgoing = dc.indexOf(cname);
if (getgoing != -1) {
getgoing += cname.length;
endit = dc.indexOf(";", getgoing);
if (endit == -1) endit = dc.length;
return unescape(dc.substring(getgoing, endit));
}
```

```
  }
  return null;
  }
  // this function saves the cookie
  function savethatCookie(name, value, until) {
  document.cookie = name + "=" + escape(value) + "; path=/" +
  ((until == null) ? "" : "; expires=" + until.toGMTString());
  }
  // this function deletes the cookie
  function getridofCookie(name) {
  document.cookie = name + "=; expires=Thu, 01-Jan-70 00:00:01 GMT" +   "; path=/";
  }
```

5. Save the document as Q2.js.

6. Open your ASCII or HTML editor and type:

```
<HTML>
<HEAD>
<SCRIPT TYPE="text/javascript" LANGUAGE="JavaScript" SRC="Q2.js"></SCRIPT>
</HEAD>
<BODY BGCOLOR = "#FFFFFF">
<SCRIPT LANGUAGE="JavaScript">
var udl = new Date();
udl.setTime(udl.getTime() + (24 * 60 * 60 * 1000 * 365));
amount=getthatCookie("visit");
if (amount==null){
document.write("Welcome, this is your first visit.");
amount++
savethatCookie("visit",amount,udl);
}
else {
```

```
document.write("Hi there again, this is your visit number
",getthatCookie("visit")," here.");
amount++;
savethatCookie("visit",amount,udl);
}
</SCRIPT>
<P><A HREF="Q2.htm#" onClick="getridofCookie('visit')">Click
here to delete the cookie</A>
</BODY>
</html>
```

7. Save the document as Q2.htm.

8. Open Q1.htm and Q2.htm in your browser.

9. Refresh the browser several times.

10. Click on the "delete the cookie" link.

11. Refresh the browser again.

A cookie set as above may look like:

```
visit
4
localhost/
0
3376884992
29529473
1352293792
29456048
*
```

Explanation

The document object contains a property called `cookie`, which in principle contains nothing more than a simple string value, normally a series of name/value pairs, e.g.:

```
document.cookie = name + "=" + escape(value)
```

results in `name = value`.

Up to 20 name/value pairs can be stored in a cookie, but a cookie can never be over 4K in size (2K or less is recommended). Cookies are created, modified, and deleted by setting the value of the cookie property. Cookies have four optional attributes: expires, path, domain, and security. If a cookie should exist beyond the browser session then expires must be set. Cookies past expiration date are automatically deleted. Cookies lifetimes are specified in milliseconds. In Example Q the value was set to one year:

```
var udl = new Date();
udl.setTime(udl.getTime() + (24 * 60 * 60 * 1000 * 365));
```

The content of the variable `udl` was set to the present time using `getTime()`, and then adding a number consisting of 365 days multiplied by 24 hours multiplied by 60 minutes multiplied by 60 seconds multiplied by 1000 to get milliseconds.

`path` specifies which web pages are allowed to read a cookie. The default behavior is files in the same directory, i.e., a cookie set in www.website.com/directory1/index.htm will be read by all files in www.website.com/directory1, but not by those in www.website.com/directory2. To get around this, `path` can be set to `/`, so that the cookie becomes visible to any page in www.website.com. In the example this can be found in the line:

```
document.cookie = name + "=" + escape(value) + "; path=/" +
```

The `domain` attribute is similar to `path`. If orders.website.com needs to read a value set in catalog.website.com, then setting `path` to `/` and `domain` to `.website.com` makes that cookie available to all servers in the website.com domain.

Secure is a Boolean value of default value 0, but which, when set to 1, will allow transmission only when browser and server are connected by HTTPS or other secure protocol.

In Example Q, upon opening the file JavaScript checks the value of the variable called amount. The variable is contained in the cookie, so if the cookie has not been set then the value contained in the variable will be non-existent (void, or null):

```
if (amount==null){
document.write("Welcome, this is your first visit.");
```

However, if the cookie has previously been set then the variable exists. The number it contains can be written to the screen and the value in the variable subsequently incremented, and the new information written again to the cookie.

```
else {
document.write("Hi again, this is your visit number " +
getthatCookie("visit") + " to this site.");
amount++;
savethatCookie("visit",amount,udl);
```

The else statement invokes the function getthatCookie, which is composed of:

```
function getthatCookie(name){
var cname = name + "=";
var dc = document.cookie;
if (dc.length > 0) {
                getgoing = dc.indexOf(cname);
                if (getgoing != -1) {
                            getgoing += cname.length;
                            endit = dc.indexOf(";", getgoing);
                    if (endit == -1) endit = dc.length;
                    return unescape(dc.substring(getgoing, endit));
                            }
            }
```

which assigns variables. The heart of the code is `document.cookie` (the cookie property of the object document), which is the code that makes the cookie. The standard function `indexOf()` searches the given string (in the first case, the content of the variable `getgoing`; in the second case, the content of the variable `endit`) from beginning to end to see if it contains an occurrence of a substring. It returns the position of the first occurrence that appears after the start position, or -1 if no such occurrence is found.

The JavaScript functions `escape()` and `unescape()` are not totally needed, but are added because there may be whitespace (spacebar character) in the information, and this character (as well as semicolon and comma) is not allowed in cookies. `escape()` encodes a string replacing all spaces, punctuation, accented characters, and any other data that is not ASCII to the form %XX, where XX is the hexadecimal representation, thus the string in `escape("Hello World!")` is rendered as `Hello%20World%21`.

`unescape()` is the only way of correctly decoding the string so as to retain the original, so `unescape` always has to be used after `escape()`:

```
document.cookie = name + "=" + escape(value)
.... code .....
return unescape(dc.substring(getgoing, endit));
```

To delete the cookie, example Q simply calls a function:

```
<P><A HREF="#" onClick="getridofCookie('visit')">Click here to
delete
```

where `getridofCookie('visit')` specifies which cookie and

```
function getridofCookie(name) {
document.cookie = name + "=; expires=Thu, 01-Jan-70 00:00:01
GMT" +  "; path=/";
}
```

sets its time to one second after the first day of 1970 (which is the earliest date recognized, and it is therefore impossible to be older), which means that the cookie is automatically deleted.

Clearly, more information can be stored in cookies than just how often the web site has been visited.

1. To continue this example, re-open your ASCII or HTML editor and type:

```
<HTML>
<HEAD>
<SCRIPT LANGUAGE= "JavaScript">
function getthatCookie(name){
var cname = name + "=";
var dc - document.cookie;
if (dc.length > 0) {
getgoing = dc.indexOf(cname);
if (getgoing != -1) {
getgoing += cname.length;
endit = dc.indexOf(";", getgoing);
if (endit == -1) endit = dc.length;
return unescape(dc.substring(getgoing, endit));
}
}
return null;
}
function savethatCookie(name, value, until) {
document.cookie = name + "=" + escape(value) + "; path=/" +
((until == null) ? "" : "; expires=" + until.toGMTString());
}
function getridofCookie(name) {
document.cookie = name + "=; expires=Thu, 01-Jan-70 00:00:01 GMT" +  "; path=/";
}
var udl = new Date();
```

```
udl.setTime(udl.getTime() +  (24 * 60 * 60 * 1000 * 365));
</SCRIPT>
<title>Cookies - remember name and color</title>
</HEAD>
<BODY BGCOLOR = "#FFFFFF">
<H2>set a cookie</H2>
<FORM NAME="savethatCookieform"
onSubmit="savethatCookie(this.saveit.value,this.savecolor.value,udl);">
What is your name: <INPUT TYPE=TEXT NAME="saveit"><BR>
Your favorite JavaScript color: <INPUT TYPE=TEXT NAME="savecolor"><BR>
<INPUT TYPE=SUBMIT VALUE="set cookie">
</FORM>
<BR>
<H2>Collect the cookie again</H2>
<FORM NAME="getthatCookieform"
onSubmit="document.bgColor=getthatCookie(this.getit.value);return false;">
Write your name: <INPUT TYPE=TEXT NAME="getit"><BR>
<INPUT TYPE=SUBMIT VALUE="get the cookie">
</FORM>
</BODY>
</html>
```

2. Save the document as Q3.htm.

3. Open Q3.htm in your browser.

4. Write your favorite JavaScript color and save the cookie.

5. Click on "collect the cookie."

Explanation

As above, examining the cookie will show that the data has actually been written to the file, e.g.:

```
Rob
blue
localhost/
0
1491983104
29529476
3883159200
29456050
*
```

Notice that onSubmit has the ability to stop the form being submitted, and is therefore ideal for performing validation checks, e.g.:

```
function checkForm(form)
{ if (form.message.value != "") return true;
else
    {
    alert("you have not written anything.");
    form.message.focus();
    return false;
    }
}
</SCRIPT>
<FORM NAME = "theform" onSubmit = "return checkForm(this)"
METHOD=POST ACTION = "/cgi-bin/formmail.etc">
<TEXTAREA NAME = "message"></TEXTAREA><P>
<INPUT TYPE = SUBMIT VALUE = "Go">
</FORM>
```

For more information on submitting forms and dynamic forms, see Example U.

VBSCRIPT

JavaScript is the standard and default script for client-side scripting. Disregarding version conflicts (e.g., that Netscape Navigator 3 will accept JavaScript 1, but not all of JavaScript 1.2), JavaScript will work in all browsers. Other languages can also be specified; however, this is not a guarantee that it will work all the time. The most widely-used alternative scripting language is VBScript. VBScript is very popular because it is in principle a simplified edition of Visual Basic and relatively easy to use. The following is a comparison of JavaScript and VBScript. Here is a JavaScript code block:

```
<SCRIPT LANGUAGE="JAVASCRIPT">
window.alert("choose what to do");
place = window.prompt("Do you want a book ? ", "Franklin Beedle");
if (place != null)
{
if (place == "Franklin Beedle")
{ gotourl = "http://www.fbeedle.com" }
else
{ gotourl = "http://www.abfcontent.com" };
window.status = "OK, we are going to " + gotourl;
if (window.confirm("get ready"))
{ window.navigate(gotourl) }
}
</SCRIPT>
```

and here is the same code block in VBScript:

```
<SCRIPT LANGUAGE="VBSCRIPT">
window.alert "choose what to do."
Dim place, gotourl
place = window.prompt("Do you want a book ?", "Franklin Beedle")
If place <> "" Then
   If place = "Franklin Beedle" Then
```

```
    gotourl = "http://www.fbeedle.com"
  Else
    gotourl  = "http://www.abfcontent.com"
  End If
  window.status = " OK, we are going to " & gotourl
  If window.confirm("get ready") Then
    window.navigate gotourl
  End If
End If
</SCRIPT>
```

In the above, significant differences are encountered in the command syntax. VBScript lacks brackets `()` and semicolons `(;)`, and commands are not grouped in curly braces `{}`. Furthermore, the familiar If/Else takes the form of IF/Then/Else/End If. Other differences include the check that the variable `place` contains a value:

```
if (place != null)
```

is replaced by checking if the content is either greater than or smaller than (inequality; `<>`) to empty:

```
If place <> ""
```

Further explanations about VBScript can be found in my book, *ASP: Learning by Example.*

Example R: Data-binding using Dynamic VBScript

In this example an HTML file will be connected to a TXT database using the <OBJECT> tag (unfortunately not supported by Netscape) and the data read using VBScript. First write the database.

1. Open your ASCII editor and type:

```
Film;Genre;Comments
When Hunky met Silly;Comedy;Great film but not very intellectual
The Gut, the Bit and the Bulky;Western;Classic, watch the eyebrows twitching
Under the Lead Lantern;Chinese;Excellent for opera buffs
Breaking the Whales;Dogma;Hand-held camera, so take sea-sickness pills
Monald Muck;Cartoon;See Monald's girlfriend, Maisy
```

2. Save the document as R.txt.

3. Open your ASCII or HTML editor and type:

```
<HTML>
<HEAD>
<TITLE>Film Browser</TITLE>
</HEAD>
<BODY>
<FORM>
<TABLE WIDTH=100%>
<TR>
<TH COLSPAN=2><BIG> Film Browser </BIG><P></TH>
</TR>
<TR>
<TD WIDTH="30%" ALIGN=RIGHT> Film Name: </TD>
<TD WIDTH="70%"> <INPUT TYPE="TEXT" SIZE="40" DATASRC="#film" DATAFLD="film"> </TD>
</TR>
<TR>
<TD ALIGN=RIGHT> Genre: </TD>
<TD> <INPUT TYPE="TEXT" SIZE="40" DATASRC="#film" DATAFLD="Genre"> </TD>
</TR>
<TR>
<TD ALIGN=RIGHT> Comments: </TD>
```

```
<TD> <INPUT TYPE="TEXT" SIZE="40" DATASRC="#film"
DATAFLD="Comments"> </TD>
</TR>
</TABLE><P>
<TABLE WIDTH=100%>
<TR>
<TD ALIGN=CENTER>
<INPUT NAME="First" TYPE="BUTTON" VALUE="Beginning">
<INPUT NAME="Previous" TYPE="BUTTON" VALUE=" < move up the list">
<INPUT NAME="Next" TYPE="BUTTON" VALUE=" > move down the list">
<INPUT NAME="Last" TYPE="BUTTON" VALUE="End">
</TD>
</TR>
</TABLE>
</FORM>
<SCRIPT LANGUAGE=VBSCRIPT>

Sub First_onclick()
film.recordset.moveFirst
End Sub

Sub Last_onclick()
film.recordset.moveLast
End Sub

Sub Previous_onclick()
If Not film.recordset.bof Then film.recordset.movePrevious
End Sub
```

```
Sub Next_onclick()
If Not film.recordset.eof Then film.recordset.moveNext
End Sub

</SCRIPT>
<OBJECT ID="film" WIDTH=100 HEIGHT=51
CLASSID="CLSID:333C7BC4-460F-11D0-BC04-0080C7055A83">
<PARAM NAME="FieldDelim" VALUE=";">
<PARAM NAME="DataURL" VALUE="R.txt">
<PARAM NAME="UseHeader" VALUE=True>
</OBJECT>
</BODY>
</HTML>
```

2. Save the document as R.htm.

3. Open R.htm in your browser.

4. Click on the various possibilities.

Explanation

The data connector control can either be of the *Simple Tabular Data* (STD) type or the *Remote Data Service* (RDS) type. RDS is used for ODBC-equipped data sources, so, as the example here only uses simple tabular data, we specify STD in the connection; the <OBJECT> tag. Here it is given an ID of film, the database is specified as R.txt (dataURL), the delimiter for each data field is defined as semicolon (it could also be commas, but commas occur in the text strings), and a further parameter defines UseHeader as being set to True. This is so that the field names in the first line of R.txt can be related to the fields we wish to view in R.htm:

```
<OBJECT ID="film" WIDTH=100 HEIGHT=51
CLASSID="CLSID:333C7BC4-460F-11D0-BC04-0080C7055A83">
```

```
<PARAM NAME="FieldDelim" VALUE=";">
<PARAM NAME="DataURL" VALUE="R.txt">
<PARAM NAME="UseHeader" VALUE=True>
</OBJECT>
```

Once the page has been opened, the browser will collect the data from the data source (dataURL) and store this in a tabular Recordset in the PC's RAM. Since this object uses ActiveX controls, the ClassID is also specified. This is the unique registry value that identifies the control, or simply the coordinates where it is on a PC.

Having acquired the data it can be shown:

```
<INPUT TYPE="TEXT" SIZE="40" DATASRC="#film" DATAFLD="film">
```

Here two items of information are provided. Notice that film is the ID of the STD. To refer to this data source, a pound (#) character has to be used. The second item is the dataField name (e.g., film).

Navigation around the data is provided by VBScript. To move through the records in the recordset, objects and methods of the STD are used. These are referred to using dot syntax, e.g., film.recordset refers to the recordset property of the object film. VBScript contains *procedures*. These are divided into functions (like JavaScript functions) and *subprocedures*. Subprocedures are declared using Sub and ended using End Sub. The code between Sub and End Sub can be executed using the method Call or any other specified event. In Example Q, the code is executed after onClick on the appropriate object.

```
<INPUT NAME="First" TYPE="BUTTON" VALUE="Beginning">
```

Thus, an onClick on the object with name First will activate:

```
<SCRIPT LANGUAGE=VBSCRIPT>
Sub First_onClick()
film.recordset.moveFirst
End Sub
```

resulting in an imaginary cursor moving to the first (topmost) row of the Recordset table using the recordset object's `moveFirst` method. The same principle applies to `moveLast`.

Clicking on the object TYPE=`"BUTTON"` with NAME =`"Previous"` will execute the code:

```
Sub Previous_onclick()
If Not film.recordset.bof Then film.recordset.movePrevious
End Sub
```

where `bof` (Beginning Of File) is first checked. If the cursor is already standing at the beginning of the file, then the method `movePrevious` will result in an error. Therefore, `movePrevious` is invoked only when the condition `If Not . . . bof` is fulfilled. The same principle applies to `moveNext`, where `eof` (End Of File) has to be checked.

DYNAMIC STYLES

Up to now CSS (Examples A–H) and JavaScript (Examples I–Q) have been kept separate. However, combining these with DOM results in a powerful technique called "Dynamic Styles." As an extension of Example Q (Q3.htm), we can see that giving variables a value, and then using that in a dynamic style, can result in a useful interactive effect.

Example S: DOM: Specifying the Background Color

1. Open your HTML or ASCII editor and type:

```
<HTML>
<HEAD>
<script language="javascript">
function start()
{
```

```
var inputColor = prompt("write which JavaScript color this
page shall be", "");
document.body.style.backgroundColor = inputColor;
}
</script>
</HEAD>
<body onLoad="start()">
<P><b>Welcome to the Web Site, what a nice color !</b></p>
</BODY>
</HTML>
```

2. Save the file as S.htm.

3. Open S.htm in your browser.

4. Input a JavaScript color.

5. Click the prompt box OK button.

Explanation

A function `start()` is defined and is called when <BODY> loads. This function opens a prompt box containing the text "write which color the page shall be" as well as two empty quotation marks. These empty quotation marks are the value of the variable `inputColor`. Obviously, if you write Red, or Cornflowerblue, or any other color in the box, then this will become the value of the variable `inputColor`. If the two empty quotation marks were not there for us to write in, then the variable's initial value would simply be undefined until we changed it. When you click the prompt box OK button, then this value (Red or whatever) is set to `document.body.style.backgroundColor`. This is because the function is written in JavaScript. JavaScript will find the largest element in the present environment (in this case, the document), and orient itself according to that. Starting from document we can define the element body, from body we can define Style and the attribute backgroundColor. Thus, <body bgcolor> is set to the value of the variable inputColor, which we have just typed in.

The use of CSS and DOM syntax here is undoubtedly much more elegant than writing the whole effect in JavaScript using lines similar to:

```
document.write("<body bgcolor=" + inputColor + ">");
```

JAVASCRIPT COLORS

There are 140 JavaScript colors, but be very careful before you use papayawhip, lightgoldenrod-yellow, blanchedalmond, etc. The 16 JavaScript "primary colors" can be used with relative impunity. These are:

Color Name	Hexadecimal Code	Color Name	Hexadecimal Code
Black	#000000	Green	#008000
Silver	#C0C0C0	Lime	#00FF00
Gray	#808080	Olive	#808000
White	#FFFFFF	Yellow	#FFFF00
Maroon	#800000	Navy	#000080
Red	#FF0000	Blue	#0000FF
Purple	#800080	Teal	#008080
Fuchia	#FF00FF	Aqua	#00FFFF

Be aware that the pound (#) sign is not used when using JavaScript colors (the # sign is only used to donate the hexadecimal values). So color = "black" is the same as color = "#000000", but color = "#black" is incorrect.

Example T: Dynamic Positioning

Just as in dynamic styles, dynamic positioning can be used by declaring the position attributes (absolute, relative, top, left, right, bottom, as well as clip, overflow, and z-index) of CSS elements.

1. Open your ASCII or HTML editor and type:

```
<HTML>
<HEAD>
<STYLE type="text/CSS">
#thediv {position:absolute;
top:100px;left:100px;width:100px;height:100px;background-color:red;border:ridge}
</STYLE>
<SCRIPT LANGUAGE="Javascript">
<!--
function WhereAmI()
{
document.theform.xfield.value = window.event.x;
document.theform.yfield.value = window.event.y;
}
function putBox()
{
thediv.style.posLeft = window.event.x - 50;
thediv.style.posTop = window.event.y - 50;
}
// -->
</SCRIPT>
</HEAD>
<BODY onMouseMove="WhereAmI();" onClick="putBox();" STYLE="cursor:hand">
<DIV ID="thediv">Div layer here</DIV>
<FORM name="theform">
The cursor's X axis position is: <input type="text" size="25" name="xfield"><BR>
```

```
The cursor's Y axis position is: <input type="text" size="25"
name="yfield">
</FORM>
</BODY>
</HTML>
```

2. Save the document as T1.htm.

3. Open T1.htm in your browser.

4. Move the mouse around the screen, clicking at random points.

Explanation

The <BODY> contains two text input fields in a <FORM> called theform. Regarded as objects, these are document.theform.xfield and document.theform.yfield. After the function WhereAmI has been called (and it is in the body statement, so it is called upon loading), then these variables are assigned numerical values corresponding to window.event.x (the X axis position of the cursor on the screen) and window.event.y (the Y axis position of the cursor on the screen) for a certain event. In this case, it is when onMouseMove happens. Clicking on the screen (which is the same as clicking on the <BODY>) calls the function putBox:

```
onClick="putBox();"
```

which equates the value of the DIV layer to the appropriate window.event coordinate (X or Y) minus 50 pixels. The reason for subtracting the 50px is because the DIV "box" is 100 by 100, so subtracting 50 makes it centered around the click position.

```
thediv.style.posLeft = window.event.x - 50;
```

The other new feature introduced in T1.htm is:

```
STYLE="cursor:hand"
```

which changes how the mouse cursor position appears. Cursor shapes can be `auto` (the default setting), `crosshair`, `hand`, `move`, `text`, `wait`, `help`, `e-resize`, `ne-resize`, `nw-resize`, `n-resize`, `se-resize`, `sw-resize`, `s-resize`, or `w-resize`.

Dynamic Positioning is a theme that can be built on. In the next example, a slight variation is shown, and the cookie file (Q2.js) from Example Q is recycled to store the page layout.

1. To continue this example, re-open your ASCII or HTML editor and type:

```
<HTML>
<HEAD>
<SCRIPT TYPE="text/javascript"
LANGUAGE="JavaScript" SRC="Q2.js">
</SCRIPT>
<STYLE type="text/css">
#theDiv1 {background:red;
    width:100;
    height:100;
    position:absolute;
    top:100;
    left:400;
    z-index: 1}
#theDiv2 {background:green;
    width:100;
    height:100;
    position:absolute;
    top:250;
    left:400;
    z-index: 1}
#theDiv3 {background:blue;
    width:100;
    height:100;
    position:absolute;
    top:400;
    left:400 ;
    z-index: 1}
</STYLE>
<SCRIPT language="Javascript">
diffX=0;
diffY=0;
var buttonDown = "no"
chooseObj=null;
function buttonDowne()
{
    chooseObject=event.srcElement;
    chooseObject.style.zIndex=2;
```

```
        diffX = window.event.x - chooseObject.style.posLeft;
        diffY = window.event.y - chooseObject.style.posTop;
        buttonDown = 'yes';
}
function buttonUp()
{
    buttonDown="no";
    chooseObject=null;
    theDiv1.style.zIndex=1;
    theDiv2.style.zIndex=1;
    theDiv3.style.zIndex=1;
}
function moveMe()
{
    if (buttonDown == "yes")
    {
    if (chooseObject!=null)
    {
            chooseObject.style.posLeft = window.event.x-diffX;
    chooseObject.style.posTop = window.event.y-diffY;
    }
    }
}
function placeElements()
{ if (getthatCookie("box1l")!=null) {
        theDiv1.style.posLeft = getthatCookie("box1l");
        theDiv1.style.posTop = getthatCookie("box1t");
        theDiv2.style.posLeft = getthatCookie("box2l");
        theDiv2.style.posTop = getthatCookie("box2t");
        theDiv3.style.posLeft = getthatCookie("box3l");
```

```
        theDiv3.style.posTop = getthatCookie("box3t");
    }
}
function savePlacements()
{
    savethatCookie("box1l",theDiv1.style.posLeft,udl)
    savethatCookie("box1t",theDiv1.style.posTop,udl)
    savethatCookie("box2l",theDiv2.style.posLeft,udl)
    savethatCookie("box2t",theDiv2.style.posTop,udl)
    savethatCookie("box3l",theDiv3.style.posLeft,udl)
    savethatCookie("box3t",theDiv3.style.posTop,udl)
}
</SCRIPT>
</HEAD>
<BODY onMouseMove="moveMe();" onMouseUp="buttonUp();" onLoad="placeElements()">
<DIV ID="theDiv1" onMouseDown="buttonDowne();" STYLE="top:100;left:400;"></DIV>
<DIV ID="theDiv2" onMouseDown="buttonDowne();" STYLE="top:250;left:400;"></DIV>
<DIV ID="theDiv3" onMouseDown="buttonDowne();" STYLE="top:400;left:400;"></DIV>
<A HREF="javascript:savePlacements()">Click here to save placing in cookie</A>
</BODY>
</HTML>
```

2. Save the document as T2.htm.

3. Open T2.htm in your browser.

4. Move one or more of the DIV layers (release the mouse to stop).

5. Refresh the browser, the DIV layers resume their original position.

6. Move one or more of the DIV layers, click to save the cookie.

7. Move a different DIV layer.

8. Refresh the browser. The one you moved before saving the cookie is now at the new position, but the one you moved after saving the cookie resumes its original position.

Remember that when testing this example you may have to remove previously-set cookies by deleting them from C:\windows\cookies and/or C:\windows\temporary internet files.

Explanation

Upon loading the <BODY>, the function placeElements is called:

```
onLoad="placeElements()"
```

which checks that the variable box11 exists or not by examining whether or not it is equal to void:

```
function placeElements()
{ if (getthatCookie("box11")!=null) {
theDiv1.style.posLeft = getthatCookie("box11");
```

If it is not equal to void, then the positions of the various DIV elements are set to the value of the variables read from the cookie. The function savePlacements, placed inline in the link, follows the reverse of this process, writing the positions to the cookie.

File T2.htm introduces onMouseUp and onMouseDown, whose functions should be clear, especially in the light of onMouseMove, as seen in S1.htm.

T2.htm also revisits the theme of Z-index (introduced in Example E): When moving elements around a page they will sometimes collide, overlap, or even completely coincide. So which one should be shown on "top of a stack"? If no object is active, then Z-index order will be followed. Z-index's default is 0, a value that the active object assumes, and thus should always be on top. Z-index can also be set to any positive integer, the higher the number the "lower down" it will come (the higher up = further away in the air if you were lying down on your back and were looking up from the ground). In T2.htm all the DIV objects were given Z-index values of 1. However if you overlap them and click away (so none of them are active) then you will see that they overlap in the order blue - green - red, because, where nothing else is specified (or if there is a Z-index conflict), then the order they appear in is the order they occur in the HTML code, with the first defined taking the behind position. In the code they were loaded in the order red - green - blue, so therefore are shown in the order blue - green - red).

In the placing of DIV layers, the default unit "pixels" has been used. However, it is possible to define other units (as briefly seen in Example F).

POSITIONING: LENGTH VALUE UNITS

Unit	Example	Description
em	1.5em	Elements font height
ex	1ex	Elements font X-height
px	14px	Pixel (dependent on screen resolution
in	0.75in	Inch
cm	5cm	Centimeter
mm	55mm	Millimeter
pt	10pt	Point (1/72 of an inch)
pc	1.5pc	Pica (12 points)

These can be used in combination with the attributes `left`, `top`, `height`, and `width`.

Home Exercise 2: Dynamic Graphics & Audio; Sniping at Layers

Make a shooting gallery. Make an HTML file containing a picture of yourself as a non-repeating background, and specify that the cursor should be crosshairs. INPUT boxes record the X and Y coordinates of where you are pointing your "gun." By clicking the mouse a bullet hole appears on the screen at the "click-point" and you can hear a gun shot. Repeat using a series of DIV or SPAN layers containing pictures of your friends. A suggestion to the coding for the first part is:

```
<HTML>
<HEAD>
<TITLE>Bulletholes</TITLE>
<STYLE type="text/CSS">
#theDiv {position:absolute; top:100;left:100;width:48;height:48}
body {background: url(my_picture.gif) no-repeat fixed center}
</STYLE>
<SCRIPT LANGUAGE="JavaScript">
<!--
function whereAmI()
{
   document.theForm.xfield.value = window.event.x;
   document.theForm.yfield.value = window.event.y;
}
function placeElements()
{
   theDiv.style.posLeft = window.event.x - 24;
   theDiv.style.posTop = window.event.y - 24;
   revolver.src = "gun.wav"
}
// -->
</SCRIPT>
<bgsound src="empty.wav" id="revolver">
```

```
</HEAD>
<BODY onMouseMove="whereAmI();" onClick="placeElements();"
STYLE="cursor:crosshair;background-color:black">
<DIV ID="theDiv"><IMG SRC="bullethole.gif" width="48"
height="48"></DIV>
<FORM name="theForm">
I am pointing at X: <input type="text" size="25"
name="xfield"><BR>
I am pointing at Y: <input type="text" size="25" name="yfield">
</FORM>
<center>
<h2 style="font-family:verdana;color:white;
letter-spacing:.5em;text-transform:uppercase;">snipe away</h2>
</center>
</BODY>
</HTML>
```

You can make your own GIF and WAV files. You can download the ones mentioned above (apart from my_picture.gif), together with coding suggestions, from the web support for this book at **www.fbeedle.com/83-x.html**. They are in a folder marked "homeX2."

Audio files are a thorn in the side of web programmers due partly to their size (and therefore download time), and partly due to the fact that playback is dependent on which plug-ins the client has installed. There are two general HTML codes for specifying audio formats; <BGSOUND> starts playing immediately after loading, e.g.:

```
<html>
<body>
<bgsound src="gun.wav" loop="5">
</body>
</html>
```

or <EMBED>, which will play once and present the plug-in's control panel on the screen, so be aware of height and width parameters. Thus:

```
<embed name="sound" src="gun.wav" height="250" width="250"
pluginurl="http://manufacturer.com/plugin/installfile.exe">
</embed>
```

PLUGINURL is not essential, but will be visited by the browser should a plug-in for that file type not be available.

Example U: Dynamic Forms

Email is the most usual method of interactivity on a web site. Email can be generated by invoking SMTP protocol using (mailto) links like:

```
<a href="mailto:info@targetsite.com?subject=I have just
finished reading about DHTML&body=it was fun"> this </a>.
```

where extra information can be added using ?subject= as well as &body=.

However, not all clients have email programs associated with their browser, and the amount of information sent is still limited; in fact, you define it yourself. Therefore, the preferred method is using <FORM>. Here is a quick refresher on FORM:

```
<form name="form1" method="post"
action="http://www.hemsida.com/cgi/sendmail/sendmail">
input type="hidden" name="recipient" value="me@myemail.com"
<!-- put your mail address in here -->
<input type="hidden" name="subject" value="results of my first
email form">
<input type="hidden" name="redirect"
value="http://www.mywebsite.com/followuppage.htm">
</form>
```

The form method is POST (it could otherwise be GET) and it calls (ACTION) an absolutely-defined Perl script on the server www.hemsida.com, which in turn points to that server's email gateway. The first (hidden) input RECIPIENT tells the email gateway whom to send the mail to, the second (hidden) input adds the string "results of my first email form" in the SUBJECT part of the email. The third hidden input tells the server to redirect the user's browser to a new page once the mail has been sent. According to type of server the form is being serviced on RECIPIENT can also be called TO. REDIRECT can also be called either MARK, FOLLOWUPPAGE, or NextURL, while SUBJECT may be shortened to SUB.

`<input type="hidden" name="cc" value="copy@server.com">` results in a copy (CC) of the email also being sent to a second address. Further email addresses can be typed in, separated (concatenated) by a comma.

The first part of Example U shows how to make the form more dynamic, and also gather a little more client information.

1. Open your ASCII or HTML editor and type:

```
<html>
<head>
<script language="JavaScript">
function gatherClientInfo()
{
document.theForm.browser.value = navigator.appName
document.theForm.bversion.value = navigator.appVersion
}
</script>
</head>
<body onLoad="document.theForm.name.focus()">
<form name="theForm" method="post" onSubmit="gatherClientInfo()"
action="http://www.hemsida.com/cgi/sendmail/sendmail">
<!-- or any other available script pointing at a mail gateway -->
<INPUT type="hidden" name="recipient" value="yourmail@yourdomain.com">
<!-- put in your email address -->
<input type="hidden" name="browser">
```

```
<input type="hidden" name="bversion">
<table border=0>
<tr><td>
Name: </td><td><input type="text" name="name"
onFocus="this.style.backgroundColor='orange'"
onBlur="this.style.backgroundColor='white'">
</td></tr>
<tr><td>
Address: </td><td><input type="text" name="address"
onFocus="this.style.backgroundColor='orange'"
onBlur="this.style.backgroundColor='white'">
</td></tr>
<tr><td>
Zip: </td><td><input type="text" name="zip"
onFocus="this.style.backgroundColor='orange'"
onBlur="this.style.backgroundColor='white'">
</td></tr>
<tr><td>
Town: </td><td><input type="text" name="town"
onFocus="this.style.backgroundColor='orange'"
onBlur="this.style.backgroundColor='white'">
</td></tr>
<tr><td>
Telephone Number: </td><td><input type="text" name="phonenr"
onFocus="this.style.backgroundColor='orange'"
onBlur="this.style.backgroundColor='white'">
</td></tr>
<tr><td> </td><td><input type=submit value="send">
<input type=reset></td></tr>
</form>
```

```
</body>
```

2. Save the document as U1.htm.

3. Open U1.htm in your browser.

4. Fill in the INPUT fields (you can also click on "send" if you wish).

Explanation

Upon loading, the cursor is moved to the first input field, called name:

```
<body onLoad="document.theForm.name.focus()">
```

For each field, Focus (and its opposite, Blur) are defined:

```
onFocus="this.style.backgroundColor='orange'"
onBlur="this.style.backgroundColor='white'">
```

Upon submitting (onSubmit), the function gatherClientInfo is called:

```
<form name="theForm" method="post" onSubmit="gatherClientInfo()"
```

which checks the client's browser:

```
function gatherClientInfo()
{
document.theForm.browser.value = navigator.appName
document.theForm.bversion.value = navigator.appVersion
}
```

(see Example P for more information on browser parameters) and puts variables into the hidden fields for sending with the mail:

```
<input type="hidden" name="browser">
<input type="hidden" name="bversion">
```

Please note that the form action sends the content of the mail (the data in the various input fields) to third-party script:

```
action="http://www.hemsida.com/cgi/sendmail/sendmail">
```

At the earliest possible opportunity, you should replace this line. If possible, replace it with your own sendmail, formmail, or similar script, because using other people's scripts is regarded as bad "Netiquette."

The next simple script shows how to check that the fields have actually been filled in.

1. To continue this example, re-open your ASCII or HTML editor and type:

```
<HTML>
<HEAD>
<TITLE>Form check - simple</TITLE>
</HEAD>
<BODY BGCOLOR = "#FFFFFF">
<SCRIPT LANGUAGE = "JavaScript">
<!--
function checkForm(form)
{
    if (form.message.value != "") return true;
    else
    {
    alert("please write something.");
    form.message.focus();
    return false;
    }
}
//-->
</SCRIPT>
<FORM onSubmit = "return checkForm(this)" METHOD=POST ACTION = "/cgi-bin/">
<TEXTAREA NAME = "message" ROWS = 6 COLS = 20 WRAP></TEXTAREA><P>
<INPUT TYPE = SUBMIT VALUE = "  Send  ">
<INPUT TYPE = RESET VALUE = "  Reset  ">
</FORM>
</BODY>
```

```
</html>
```

2. Save the document as U2.htm.

3. Open U2.htm in your browser.

Explanation

This is the heart of a <FORM> fields check. As seen before, `onSubmit` can return `True` or `False`, and thus can stop the form submission process.

```
<FORM onSubmit = "return checkForm(this)" METHOD=POST ACTION = "/cgi-bin/">
```

calls the function and checks what it returns. The function returns true if the variable `message` in the form has content (not equal to void), and thus the message is sent:

```
if (form.message.value != "") return true;
```

Otherwise the function will return false. This stops the message and opens an alert box containing a string literal:

```
alert("please write something.");
    form.message.focus();
    return false;
```

and move the focus back to the <INPUT> type. In this case the <INPUT> type is <TEXTAREA>, but could just as well have been another type of input.

The following is a little more complicated.

1. To continue this example, re-open your ASCII or HTML editor and type:

```
<HTML>
<HEAD><TITLE>Form check - avanced</TITLE>
<SCRIPT LANGUAGE = "JavaScript">
function isFilled(element) {
    if (element.value == "" ||
```

```
                    element.value == null)
          return false;
          else return true;
}
function isEmail(element) {
          if (element.value.indexOf("@") + "" != "-1" &&
              element.value.indexOf(".") + "" != "-1" &&
              element.value != "")
          return true;
          else return false;
}
function isReady(form) {
       if (isFilled(form.name) == false) {
       alert("please write your name");
       form.name.focus();
       return false;
       }
       if (isFilled(form.message) == false) {
       alert("you have forgotten to send a message.");
       form.message.focus();
       return false;
       }
       if (isEmail(form.address) == false)
       {
       alert("please write your email address.");
       form.address.focus();
       return false;
       }
    return true;
}
</SCRIPT>
```

```
</HEAD>
<BODY BGCOLOR = "#FFFFFF">
<FORM onSubmit = "return isReady(this)" ACTION = "cgi-bin/etc">
Your name: <INPUT NAME = "name" TYPE = TEXT>
Your email address: <INPUT NAME = "address" TYPE = TEXT>
<P>Your message:<P><TEXTAREA NAME = "message" ROWS = 6 COLS = 65 WRAP></TEXTAREA>
<P><INPUT TYPE = SUBMIT VALUE = " Send ">
<INPUT TYPE = RESET VALUE = " Reset ">
</FORM>
</BODY>
</html>
```

2. Save the document as U3.htm.

3. Open U3.htm in your browser.

Explanation

The form contains three inputs: name, message, and address. Upon submission, the function isReady() is called:

```
<FORM onSubmit = "return isReady(this)" ACTION = "cgi-bin/etc">
```

isReady() calls and checks further functions, amongst them isFilled():

```
function isReady(form) {
    if (isFilled(form.name) == false) {
```

isFilled() takes an element which has been named and checks to see if the content has no content, and if it indeed has no content, then equates it to void and returns false.

```
function isFilled(element) {
    if (element.value == "" ||
        element.value == null)
    return false;
```

The `isFilled()` function for `message` is similar to that for `name`. If `isFilled()` returns true for these cases, then the function `isEmail()` is called:

```
function isEmail(element) {
    if (element.value.indexOf("@") + "" != "-1" &&
        element.value.indexOf(".") + "" != "-1" &&
        element.value != "")
    return true;
```

where the string content is checked (using `indexOf`, see Example P) to see if the occurrence of the "at" character (@) is minus one, and (logical `&&`) the occurrence of the dot (`.`) character is minus one, and also if the string is void or not. Why check for -1 ? That is because (as explained earlier) JavaScript starts to number at 0, so non-occurrence is minus one (-1). Since all email addresses contain @ and . once (and normally only once), then the email address conforms to the address syntax (although one can never check if the address is "real" and the post box is actually emptied by that person).

Clearly, it could be advantageous to check that @ does not occur twice. Other failings are that strings are checked for content, but not for which content. The above check allows you to have a name like "5" or "+". Would it not be better if more parameters were checked ? And if you have several forms on your web site, then is it not prudent to have the script centrally in one JavaScript (.js) file?

REGULAR EXPRESSIONS

`RegExp` is an object that generates instances of regular objects, which are used in locating text that matches patterns of characters or characteristics. To create a regular expression object, surround the pattern with forward slash (/) signs, and then either the whole expression can be assigned to a variable or used directly as a method parameter. For example, the following statement creates a regular expression whose pattern is a simple word:

```
var ra = /rats/
```

This expression would find "rats" as well as "catsandrats." But regular expression notations also consist of a number of *metacharacters*, which can be imagined to be shortcuts, or shorthand notation, for more complex ideas, e.g., the boundary on either side of a word, any numeral, or characters.

```
var ra = /\brats\b/
```

now specifies word boundaries on both sides, so the variable "ra" would now find only "rats." A notation list follows:

(meta)character	Matches	Example
\b	word boundary	/\bto/ matches "tommy" /to\b/ matches "potato" /\bto\b/ matches "to"
\B	word non-boundary	/\Bto/ matches "stoop" and "potato" /to\B/ matches "stoop" and "tommy" /\Bto\B/ matches "stoop"
\d	numeral 0 to 9	/\d\d/ matches "44"
\D	non-numeral	/\D\D/ matches "to"
\s	single white space	/super\sman/ matches "super man"
\S	single non-whitespace	/super\Sman/ matches "super-man"
\w	letter, numeral, or underscore	/10\w/ matches "10X"
\W	not a letter nor numeral nor underscore	/10\W/ matches "10%"
.	any character except new-line	/../ matches "X9"

(meta)character	Matches	Example *(continued)*
[ ]	any one of the characters within the brackets	/M[aeiou]y/ matches "May", or "Mey", etc.
[^]	none of the character set	/M[^eiou]y/ matches only "May"
*	zero or more times	/\d*/ matches "", "1", or "22"
?	zero or once	/\d?/ matches "", or "2"
+	one or more times	/\d+/ matches "2", or "333"
{n}	exactly n times	/\d{2}/ matches "33"
{n,}	n or more times	/\d{2,}/ matches "444"
{n,m}	at least n times and at most m times	/\d{2,4}/ matches "5555"
^	at the beginning of a string	/^Tom/ matches "Tom says ..."
$	at the end of a string	/Tom.$/ matches "Hello Tom."

Example V: Practical RegExp.

1. Open your ASCII or HTML editor and type:

```
<html>
<head>
<SCRIPT src="V.js"></SCRIPT>
</head>
<body>
<form action="V.htm" method="post" onsubmit="return check(this)">
<table>
<tr><td>First Name </td><td><input name="firstname_le"></td></tr>
<tr><td>Last Name </td><td><input name="lastname_le"></td></tr>
```

```
<tr><td>Telephone </td><td><input name="Telephone_8$nu"></td></tr>
<tr><td>Email </td><td><input name="email_em"></td></tr>
<tr><td>Address </td><td><input name="address_st"></td></tr>
<tr><td>Zip </td><td><input name="zip_4$nu"></td></tr>
<tr><td>Town </td><td><input name="town_le"></td></tr>
<tr><td colspan="2"><input type="submit"></td></tr>
</table>
</form>
</body>
</html>
```

2. Save the document as V.htm.

3. Open your ASCII or HTML editor and type:

```
function check(what) {
cycle:
for (i=0;i<what.elements.length;i++) {
fname = what.elements[i].name
if (fname.indexOf("_") != -1) {
whichOne = fname.substr(fname.length-2,2)
howMany = fname.substring(fname.indexOf("_")+1,fname.indexOf("$"))
alert(howMany) /* this checks on how far you get through the check and for all
normal purposes other than development and testing would be commented out */
if (whichOne == "em")
reg = /^[a-z]+\.?[A-Z]+@\w+\.\w{2,2}$/
else if (whichOne == "le")
reg = /^[A-Za-z\-\s]+$/
else if (whichOne == "st")
reg = /^[A-Za-z0-9,.\s]+$/
else if (whichOne = "nu") {
reg =eval("/^[0-9]{" + howMany + "}$/")
```

```
}
testing = what.elements[i].value
if (reg.test(testing))
ok = true
else {
alert("Error!\nDisallowed characters or number of characters
in : " + fname.substr(0,fname.indexOf("_")))
ok = false
break cycle
}}}
alert(ok)
//return ok
}
```

4. Save the document as V.js.

5. Open V.htm in your browser.

Explanation

Pay attention to the layout of the input field names. They are broken with an under-score:

```
<tr><td>First Name </td><td><input name="firstname_le"></td></tr>
```
or also contain a dollar ($) character:

```
<tr><td>Zip </td><td><input name="zip_4$nu"></td></tr>
```
Obviously, their exact name is not important, but the underscore (_) and dollar ($) characters are clearly flags. They are used in the JavaScript file:

```
cycle:
for (i=0;i<what.elements.length;i++) {
fname = what.elements[i].name
if (fname.indexOf("_") != -1) {
```

The loop cycle sets i=0, then checks the name and increments to accept the next name. A condition (if) tests that the name contains an underscore by checking that its occurrence is not null.

```
whichOne = fname.substr(fname.length-2,2)
```

A new variable is made containing the last two characters of the input field name. The "-2" breaks two characters from the end, and ",2" takes these two characters, and equates them to the value of the variable whichOne in that cycle of the loop. These two characters can be any convenient ones, but this example took em (for email), le (for letters), st (for string), or nu (for numbers).

A similar command takes the number before the dollar sign:

```
howMany = fname.substring(fname.indexOf("_")+1,fname.indexOf("$"))
```

and will use this later to test how many numbers have been submitted. The tests for content invoke regular expressions. Those readers used to Perl (*Practical Extraction and Reporting Language*) will recognize the following type of code:

```
reg = /^[a-z]+\.?[a-z]+@\w+\.\w{2,2}$/
```

For those not familiar with Perl, it is the language often used in CGI (*Common General Interface*) scripts. However, to explain the JavaScript code:

- / opens the expression

- ^ says no characters (except the following):

    - plus (+) one or more times (\ .), any character except new-line (?), zero or once, or

    - /^[a-z]+\.?

This is followed by an @ sign, followed by any letter, numeral, or underscore (\w), and then a full stop (.) where there are at least two letters, numerals, or underscores before the point (.) and at least two afterwards ($ = at end of string):

```
[a-z]+@\w+\.\w{2,2}$/
```

Similarly:

```
/^[A-Za-z0-9,.\s]+$/
```

means any letter from a to z, plus any letter from A to Z (capitals), plus any numeral from 0 to 9, and plus any character except new-line but including single white space. Of course, if more characters were wanted over and above the ASCII character set, then they can be specified too. For example, Danish has three "extra" letters, æ, ø, and å, which occur both as capitals (upper case) and small (lower case) letters. These are simply added as appropriate:

```
/^[A-ZÆØÅa-zæøå0-9,.\s]+$/
```

Likewise, umlaut, circumflex, and other characters can be added as appropriate.

Home Exercise 3: onFocus, onBlur, and Regular Expressions

Re-read the code in V.js and V.htm, then re-write V.js to be more efficient. Remember it is annoying for people with European telephone numbers to be rejected from a U. S. web site because the FORM check is written too narrowly. Think of all the factors you can and then use regular expressions to check the content. However, also remember that it is impossible to check that an email or a telephone number actually exists (think about how you could check that) and/or that it is that person which actually gets the message. Use Focus and Blur to change the input field color (see T1.htm) as the form is being filled out. The check should also return the user to fields that have been improperly filled out or left blank, and these fields are now colored red.

Example W: Drop-down Menus

1. Open your ASCII or HTML editor and type:

```
<HTML>
<HEAD>
<TITLE>Menu System 1</TITLE>
<SCRIPT language="JavaScript">
IsMenu1Open=false;
menutimer1=null;
function OpenMenu1()
{
    CloseMenu2();
    if (IsMenu1Open==false)
    { // drop the menu down
      posy=Menu1.style.posTop+32;
      Menu1.style.posTop=posy;
```

```
        if (posy<16)
        { clearTimeout(menutimer1);
           menutimer1=setTimeout("OpenMenu1()",25);
        }
        else
        IsMenu1Open=true;
    }
}
function Close1()
{
    if (IsMenu1Open)
    { Menu1.style.posTop=-112;
        IsMenu1Open=false;
    }
}

IsMenu2Open=false;
menutimer2=null;
function OpenMenu2()
{
    Close1();
    if (IsMenu2Open==false)
    {
        posy=Menu2.style.posTop+32;
        Menu2.style.posTop=posy;
        if (posy<16)
        { clearTimeout(menutimer2);
           menutimer2=setTimeout("OpenMenu2()",25);
        }
        else
        IsMenu2Open=true;
```

```
        }
    }
    function CloseMenu2()
    {
        if (IsMenu2Open)
        {   Menu2.style.posTop=-112;
            IsMenu2Open=false;
        }
    }
    function OpenClose1()
    {
        if (IsMenu1Open)
            Close1();
        else
            OpenMenu1();
    }
    function OpenCloseMenu2()
    {
        if (IsMenu2Open)
            CloseMenu2();
        else
            OpenMenu2();
    }
    </SCRIPT>
    </HEAD>
    <BODY bgColor=#707070>
    <DIV id=topbar style="PADDING-RIGHT: 2px; PADDING-LEFT: 2px;
    Z-INDEX: 3; LEFT: 0px; PADDING-BOTTOM: 2px; WIDTH: 100%;
    PADDING-TOP: 2px; POSITION: absolute; TOP: 0px; HEIGHT: 16px;
    BACKGROUND-COLOR: #000000">
```

```
<A id=MenuName1 onmouseover="MenuName1.style.color='#ffff00'"
style="FONT-SIZE: 12px; COLOR: #a0a0a0; FONT-FAMILY: verdana;
TEXT-DECORATION: none" onfocus=this.blur()
onmouseout="MenuName1.style.color='#a0a0a0'"
href="javascript:OpenClose1()">Menu 1</A>

<A id=MenuName2 onmouseover="MenuName2.style.color='#ffff00'"
style="FONT-SIZE: 12px; LEFT: 30px; COLOR: #a0a0a0;
FONT-FAMILY: verdana; POSITION: relative;
TEXT-DECORATION: none" onfocus=this.blur()
onmouseout="MenuName2.style.color='#a0a0a0'"
href="javascript:OpenCloseMenu2()">Menu 2</A></DIV>

<DIV id=Menu2 style="PADDING-RIGHT: 2px; PADDING-LEFT: 2px;
FONT-SIZE: 12px; Z-INDEX: 2; LEFT: 78px; VISIBILITY: visible;
PADDING-BOTTOM: 2px; WIDTH: 150px; COLOR: #b0b0b0;
LINE-HEIGHT: 18px; PADDING-TOP: 2px; FONT-FAMILY: verdana;
POSITION: absolute; TOP: -112px; HEIGHT: 100px;
BACKGROUND-COLOR: #202020; TEXT-DECORATION: none">
Menu2 Point1<BR>Menu2 Point2<BR>Menu2 Point3<BR>Menu2
Point4<BR>
</DIV>

<DIV id=Menu1 style="PADDING-RIGHT: 2px; PADDING-LEFT: 2px;
FONT-SIZE: 12px; Z-INDEX: 2; LEFT: 2px; VISIBILITY: visible;
PADDING-BOTTOM: 2px; WIDTH: 150px; COLOR: #b0b0b0;
LINE-HEIGHT: 18px; PADDING-TOP: 2px; FONT-FAMILY: verdana;
POSITION: absolute; TOP: -112px; HEIGHT: 100px;
BACKGROUND-COLOR: #202020; TEXT-DECORATION: none">
<A id=Menu1Point1
onmouseover="Menu1Point1.style.color='#ffff00'"
```

```
style="COLOR: #b0b0b0; TEXT-DECORATION: none"
onmouseout="Menu1Point1.style.color='#b0b0b0'"
href="http://www.fbeedle.com">Menu1 Point1</A><BR>
<A id=Menu1Point2
onmouseover="Menu1Point2.style.color='#ffff00'"
style="COLOR: #b0b0b0; TEXT-DECORATION: none"
onmouseout="Menu1Point2.style.color='#b0b0b0'"
href="http://www.fbeedle.com">Menu1 Point2</A><BR>
<A id=Menu1Point3
onmouseover="Menu1Point3.style.color='#ffff00'"
style="COLOR: #b0b0b0; TEXT-DECORATION: none"
onmouseout="Menu1Point3.style.color='#b0b0b0'"
href="http://www.fbeedle.com">Menu1 Point3</A><BR>
<A id=Menu1Point4
onmouseover="Menu1Point4.style.color='#ffff00'"
style="COLOR: #b0b0b0; TEXT-DECORATION: none"
onmouseout="Menu1Point4.style.color='#b0b0b0'"
href="http://www.fbeedle.com">Menu1 Point4</A><BR>
</DIV>

</BODY>
</HTML>
```

2. Save the document as W1.htm.

3. Open W1.htm in your browser.

4. Click on the menus.

Explanation

The BODY is divided into three DIV layers. The first (`ID = topbar`) simply specifies the top navigation bar and its style, and which contains two A HREFs. These HREFs call the functions in HEAD:

```
href="javascript:OpenCloseMenu2() etc.
```

where the function checks if that menu is open. If it is open, then it the function closes it, otherwise it is opened (if not already open):

```
function OpenCloseMenu2()
{
if (IsMenu2Open)
CloseMenu2();
else
OpenMenu2();
}
```

First it checks if the menu is open (`IsMenu2Open`) by controlling whether the position of the `Menu2` DIV layer is "up":

```
Menu2.style.posTop=-112;
IsMenu2Open=false;
```

or otherwise setting the position of the DIV layer "down":

```
posy=Menu2.style.posTop+32;
```

The timer function:

```
{ clearTimeout(menutimer1);
menutimer1=setTimeout("OpenMenu1()",25);  }
```

simply specifies a 25 millisecond interval so that the menu appears to "roll" down, and not suddenly jump into position. The resulting DIV:

```
<DIV id=Menu2
```

consists simply of HTML interspersed text:

```
Menu2 Point1<BR>Menu2 Point2<BR>Menu2 Point3<BR>Menu2 Point4<BR>
```

The other DIV, with an ID of Menu1, is simply a repeat of the simple Menu2, but here further HREFs are specified, e.g.:

```
<A id=Menu1Point1
onmouseover="Menu1Point1.style.color='#ffff00'"
style="COLOR: #b0b0b0; TEXT-DECORATION: none"
onmouseout="Menu1Point1.style.color='#b0b0b0'"
href="http://www.fbeedle.com">Menu1 Point1</A><BR>
```

where the A COLOR and TEXT-DECORATION could clearly have been specified in a STYLE block in HEAD, but are included here along with onmouseover/out (see Example Y) to illustrate a possibility of combining CSS, JavaScript, and DOM.

The next code repeats V1.htm, but it shows that many different types of DIV content are possible. Here you will need a GIF image (of yourself?) in a justified height of 97px. Obviously, you can recycle some previous image files.

1. To continue this example, re-open your ASCII or HTML editor and type:

```
<HTML>
<HEAD>
<TITLE>Menu System 2</TITLE>
<SCRIPT language="JavaScript">
IsMenu1Open=false;
menutimer1=null;
function OpenMenu1()
{
    Close2();
    Close3();
    Close4();
    if (IsMenu1Open==false)
    {  // drop the menu down
```

```
      posy=Menu1.style.posTop+32;              { clearTimeout(menutimer2);
      Menu1.style.posTop=posy;                   menutimer2=
      if (posy<16)                               setTimeout("Open2()",25);
      { clearTimeout(menutimer1);              }
        menutimer1=                            else
        setTimeout("OpenMenu1()",25);          IsMenu2Open=true;
      }                                      }
      else                             }
      IsMenu1Open=true;                 function Close2()
    }                                  {
  }                                       MenuName2.style.color='#a0a0a0';
function Close1()                          if (IsMenu2Open)
{                                          { Menu2.style.posTop=-112;
    MenuName1.style.color='#a0a0a0';          IsMenu2Open=false;
    if (IsMenu1Open)                         }
    { Menu1.style.posTop=-112;            }
      IsMenu1Open=false;
    }                                   IsMenu3Open=false;
}                                       menutimer3=null;
IsMenu2Open=false;                      function Open3()
menutimer2=null;                        {
function Open2()                           Close1();
{                                          Close2();
    Close1();                              Close4();
    Close3();
    Close4();                             if (IsMenu3Open==false)
    if (IsMenu2Open==false)               {
    {                                        posy=Menu3.style.posTop+32;
      posy=Menu2.style.posTop+32;            Menu3.style.posTop=posy;
      Menu2.style.posTop=posy;               if (posy<16)
      if (posy<16)                           { clearTimeout(menutimer3);
```

```
         menutimer3=
         setTimeout("Open3()",25);
      }
      else
      IsMenu3Open=true;
   }
}
function Close3()
{
   MenuName3.style.color='#a0a0a0';
   if (IsMenu3Open)
   {  Menu3.style.posTop=-112;
      IsMenu3Open=false;
   }
}
IsMenu4Open=false;
menutimer4=null;
function Open4()
{
   Close1();
   Close2();
   Close3();
   if (IsMenu4Open==false)
   {
      posy=Menu4.style.posTop+32;
      Menu4.style.posTop=posy;
      if (posy<16)
      { clearTimeout(menutimer4);
        menutimer4=
        setTimeout("Open4()",25);
```

```
      }
      else
      IsMenu4Open=true;
   }
}
function Close4()
{
   MenuName4.style.color='#a0a0a0';
   if (IsMenu4Open)
   {  Menu4.style.posTop=-112;
      IsMenu4Open=false;
   }
}
function OpenClose1()
{
   if (IsMenu1Open)
   Close1();
   else
   OpenMenu1();
   MenuName1.style.color='#ffff00'
}
function OpenClose2()
{
   if (IsMenu2Open)
   Close2();
   else
   Open2();
   MenuName2.style.color='#ffff00'
}
function OpenClose3()
```

```
{
   if (IsMenu3Open)
   Close3();
   else
   Open3();
   MenuName3.style.color='#ffff00'
}
function OpenClose4()
{
   if (IsMenu4Open)
   Close4();
   else
   Open4();
   MenuName4.style.color='#ffff00'
}
</SCRIPT>
</HEAD>
<BODY bgColor=#707070>
<DIV id=topbar style="PADDING-RIGHT: 2px; PADDING-LEFT: 2px;
Z-INDEX: 3; LEFT: 0px; PADDING-BOTTOM: 2px; WIDTH: 100%;
PADDING-TOP: 2px; POSITION: absolute; TOP: 0px; HEIGHT: 16px;
BACKGROUND-COLOR: #000000">

<A id=MenuName1 onmouseover=
"MenuName1.style.color='#ffff00'"
style="FONT-SIZE: 12px; COLOR: #a0a0a0; FONT-FAMILY: verdana;
TEXT-DECORATION: none" onfocus=this.blur()
onmouseout="if (!IsMenu1Open)MenuName1.style.color
='#a0a0a0'" href="javascript:OpenClose1()">
Menu 1</A>
```

```
<A id=MenuName2 onmouseover="MenuName2.style.color='#ffff00'"
style="FONT-SIZE: 12px; LEFT: 30px; COLOR: #a0a0a0;
FONT-FAMILY: verdana; POSITION: relative;
TEXT-DECORATION: none"
onfocus=this.blur()
onmouseout="if (!IsMenu2Open)MenuName2.style.color='#a0a0a0'"
href="javascript:OpenClose2()">Menu 2</A>

<A id=MenuName3 onmouseover="MenuName3.style.color='#ffff00'"
style="FONT-SIZE: 12px; LEFT: 60px; COLOR: #a0a0a0;
FONT-FAMILY: verdana; POSITION: relative;
TEXT-DECORATION: none"
onfocus=this.blur()
onmouseout="if (!IsMenu3Open)MenuName3.style.color='#a0a0a0'"
href="javascript:OpenClose3()">Photo</A>

<A id=MenuName4 onmouseover="MenuName4.style.color='#ffff00'"
style="FONT-SIZE: 12px; LEFT: 90px; COLOR: #a0a0a0;
FONT-FAMILY: verdana; POSITION: relative;
TEXT-DECORATION: none"
onfocus=this.blur()
onmouseout="if (!IsMenu4Open)MenuName4.style.color='#a0a0a0'"
href="javascript:OpenClose4();">Subscribe</A>
</DIV>

<DIV id=Menu1 style="PADDING-RIGHT: 2px; PADDING-LEFT: 2px;
FONT-SIZE: 12px; Z-INDEX: 2; LEFT: 2px; VISIBILITY: visible;
PADDING-BOTTOM: 2px; WIDTH: 150px; COLOR: #b0b0b0;
LINE-HEIGHT: 18px; PADDING-TOP: 2px; FONT-FAMILY: verdana;
POSITION: absolute; TOP: -112px; HEIGHT: 100px;
BACKGROUND-COLOR: #202020; TEXT-DECORATION: none">
```

```
<A id=Menu1Point1
onmouseover="Menu1Point1.style.color='#ffff00'"
style="COLOR: #b0b0b0; TEXT-DECORATION: none"
onmouseout="Menu1Point1.style.color='#b0b0b0'"
href="http://www.fbeedle.com">Menu1 Point1</A><BR>

<A id=Menu1Point2
onmouseover="Menu1Point2.style.color='#ffff00'"
style="COLOR: #b0b0b0; TEXT-DECORATION: none"
onmouseout="Menu1Point2.style.color='#b0b0b0'"
href="http://www.fbeedle.com">Menu1 Point2</A><BR>

<A id=Menu1Point3
onmouseover="Menu1Point3.style.color='#ffff00'"
style="COLOR: #b0b0b0; TEXT-DECORATION: none"
onmouseout="Menu1Point3.style.color='#b0b0b0'"
href="http://www.fbeedle.com">Menu1 Point3</A><BR>

<A id=Menu1Point4
onmouseover="Menu1Point4.style.color='#ffff00'"
style="COLOR: #b0b0b0; TEXT-DECORATION: none"
onmouseout="Menu1Point4.style.color='#b0b0b0'"
href="http://www.fbeedle.com">Menu1 Point4</A><BR>
</DIV>

<DIV id=Menu2 style="PADDING-RIGHT: 2px; PADDING-LEFT: 2px;
FONT-SIZE: 12px; Z-INDEX: 2; LEFT: 78px; VISIBILITY: visible;
PADDING-BOTTOM: 2px; WIDTH: 150px; COLOR: #b0b0b0;
LINE-HEIGHT: 18px; PADDING-TOP: 2px; FONT-FAMILY: verdana;
POSITION: absolute; TOP: -112px; HEIGHT: 100px;
BACKGROUND-COLOR: #202020; TEXT-DECORATION: none">
```

```
Menu2 Point1<BR>Menu2 Point2<BR>Menu2 Point3<BR>Menu2
Point4<BR>
</DIV>

<DIV id="Menu3" style="PADDING-RIGHT: 2px; PADDING-LEFT: 2px;
FONT-SIZE: 12px; Z-INDEX: 2; LEFT: 154px; VISIBILITY:
visible; PADDING-BOTTOM: 2px; WIDTH: 150px; COLOR: #b0b0b0;
LINE-HEIGHT: 18px; PADDING-TOP: 2px; FONT-FAMILY: verdana;
POSITION: absolute; TOP: -112px; HEIGHT: 100px;
BACKGROUND-COLOR: #000000; TEXT-DECORATION: none">
<CENTER><IMG height="97" src="my_picture.gif"
width="120"></CENTER>
</DIV>

<DIV id="Menu4" style="PADDING-RIGHT: 2px; PADDING-LEFT: 2px;
FONT-SIZE: 12px; Z-INDEX: 2; LEFT: 226px;
VISIBILITY: visible; PADDING-BOTTOM: 2px; WIDTH: 150px;
COLOR: #b0b0b0; LINE-HEIGHT: 18px; PADDING-TOP: 2px;
FONT-FAMILY: verdana; POSITION: absolute; TOP: -112px;
HEIGHT: 100px; BACKGROUND-COLOR: #202020;
TEXT-DECORATION: none">
<CENTER>
<FORM> <!-- notice no ACTION, to make this active, see
Example U -->
<TABLE>
<TBODY>
<TR>
<TD style="FONT-SIZE: 8px"> </TD></TR>
<TR>
<TD style="FONT-SIZE: 10px; COLOR: #b0b0b0;
FONT-FAMILY: verdana"
```

```
align="left">Email:</TD></TR>
<TR>
<TD align="middle"><INPUT TYPE="TEXT"></TD></TR>
<TR>
<TD
align="right"><INPUT type="submit" value="Subscribe">
</TD></TR></TBODY>
</TABLE>
</FORM>
</CENTER>
</DIV>
</BODY>
</HTML>
```

2. Save the document as W2.htm.

3. Open W2.htm in your browser.

4. Click on the various menus.

Explanation

As said above, DOM/CSS can be declared various ways. Notice the A HREFs include:

```
onmouseout="if (!IsMenu1Open)MenuName1.style.color='#a0a0a0'"
```

which first checks the JavaScript if statement (actually `!IF`, an `IF-NOT`) and, if the Boolean return is true, sets the text color after the mouse has traveled over the text—notice the use of single quotes (`'`) and not double quotation marks (`"`). This is actually the counterpart to the declaration in HEAD:

```
function OpenClose1()
{
    if (IsMenu1Open)
```

```
      Close1();
      else
      OpenMenu1();
      MenuName1.style.color='#ffff00'
}
```

where it can be seen that `style.color` (in the case of "open") is already given. Furthermore, note that each click on an A HREF means checking that several more menus are not open; or, in case they are open, they will have to be closed, e.g.:

```
function Open4()
{
    Close1();
    Close2();
    Close3();
```

So, as in V1.htm, the only solution is to logically check in a "tree" of IF statements; but where the DOM/STYLE should be put depends on your own taste and experience.

The code for Menu3 is:

```
<DIV id="Menu3" style="PADDING-RIGHT: 2px; PADDING-LEFT: 2px;
FONT-SIZE: 12px; Z-INDEX: 2; LEFT: 154px; VISIBILITY: visible;
PADDING-BOTTOM: 2px; WIDTH: 150px; COLOR: #b0b0b0;
LINE-HEIGHT: 18px; PADDING-TOP: 2px; FONT-FAMILY: verdana;
POSITION: absolute; TOP: -112px; HEIGHT: 100px;
BACKGROUND-COLOR: #000000; TEXT-DECORATION: none">
<CENTER><IMG height="97" src="my_picture.gif" width="120">
</CENTER>
</DIV>''
```

which simply shows the DIV style and the associated text/HTML commands. Similarly, the code for Menu4 is:

```
<DIV id="Menu4" style = "PADDING-RIGHT: 2px; PADDING-LEFT: 2px;
FONT-SIZE: 12px; Z-INDEX: 2; LEFT: 226px; VISIBILITY: visible;
PADDING-BOTTOM: 2px; WIDTH: 150px; COLOR: #b0b0b0;
LINE-HEIGHT: 18px; PADDING-TOP: 2px; FONT-FAMILY: verdana;
POSITION: absolute; TOP: -112px; HEIGHT: 100px;
BACKGROUND-COLOR: #202020; TEXT-DECORATION: none">
<CENTER>
<FORM>
<TABLE>
<TBODY>
<TR>
<TD style="FONT-SIZE: 8px"> </TD></TR>
<TR>
<TD style="FONT-SIZE: 10px; COLOR: #b0b0b0;
FONT-FAMILY: verdana" align = "left">
Email:
</TD>
</TR>
<TR>
<TD align="middle"><INPUT TYPE="TEXT"></TD></TR>
<TR>
<TD align="right"><INPUT type="submit" value="Subscribe">
</TD></TR></TBODY>
</TABLE>
</FORM>
</CENTER>
</DIV>
```

which contains a table, form, and input element. Obviously, input checks, as in
Examples U and V, could be included here.

Example X: Movement Using Timer Functions

In Example W, a timer function was used to "roll" the drop-down across the screen. Now it is time to take a closer look at such functions:

1. Open your HTML or ASCII editor and type:

```
<HTML>
<HEAD>
<script language="javascript">
var speed = 5;
var count = 10;
var firstLine = "Hello";
var fontstyle = ["serif", "courier", "arial" ]
var fontstylecount = 0
var direction
// so the various variables are defined
function start()
{
window.setInterval( "run()", 100 );
}
function run()
{
count += speed
if ( ( count % 200 ) == 0 )
{
speed *= -1;
direction = !direction;
pText.style.color = (speed < 0 ) ? "red" : "blue" ;
firstLine = ( speed < 0 ) ? "Goodbye" : "Hello";
pText.style.fontfamily = fontstyle [ ++fontstylecount % 3 ];
}
```

```
pText.style.fontSize = count / 3;
pText.style.left = count;
pText.innerHTML = firstLine + "<br> Font size: " + count
+ "px";
}
</script>
</head>
<body onLoad="start()">
<P ID = "pText" style = "position:absolute; left:0;
font-family:serif">
<!-- try also style = "position:absolute; left:0; font-
family:serif; color:blue" can you explain the difference -->
If you can see this, you are using Netscape Navigator</p>
</body>
</html>
```

2. Save the document as X1.htm.

3. Open X1.htm in your browser and let the text cycle at least three times.

Explanation

In principle, this is quite simple. As in the previous examples, the element P having the ID pText is positioned and its initial properties are set to blue Hello text. The content of this specified element is continuously updated using:

```
window.setInterval( "run()", 100 );
```

which tells which function to invoke (run()) and how often (every 100 milliseconds). Font size increments are set:

```
pText.style.fontfamily = fontstyle [ ++fontstylecount ];
```

until 200 is reached, at which time the incrementation is reversed:

```
if ( ( count % 200 ) == 0 )
{
speed *= -1;
direction = !direction;
```

The content is set to `Goodbye` and the color to red, and the results are displayed:

```
firstLine + "<br> Font size: " + count + "px"
```

Note that here (as in Example J), Netscape Navigator will not accept `innerText`, as it is not in Netscape's DOM. In the next code a more practical usage is illustrated.

1. To continue this example, re-open your ASCII or HTML editor and type:

```
<HTML>
<HEAD>
<STYLE type="text/CSS">
#mindivTop {
    position:absolute;
    top:0;left:-10;
    width:1200;
    height:200;
    background:blue
}
#mindivBottom {
    position:absolute;
    top:200;
    left:-10;
    width:1200;
    height:200;
    background:navy
}
#text {
```

```
      position:absolute;
      top:10;
      font-size:120px;
      color:teal;
      font-family:Expo, Verdana;
      letter-spacing:-6pt;
      text-align:center
}
</STYLE>
<SCRIPT language="JavaScript">
function placeElements()
{
   t = 0;
   b = document.body.clientHeight/2;
   mindivTop.style.height = document.body.clientHeight/2;
   mindivBottom.style.posTop = b;
   mindivBottom.style.height = document.body.clientHeight/2;
   text.style.width = document.body.clientWidth;
   text.style.posTop = b-80;
}
function start()
{
   mindivTop.style.posTop = t=t-5;
   mindivBottom.style.posTop = b=b+5;
   if (b<=document.body.clientHeight)
   {
      setTimeout("start()",1);
   }
   else window.status="finished";
}
</SCRIPT>
```

```
</HEAD>
<BODY BGCOLOR="silver" SCROLL="no" onClick="start()"
onResize="placeElements()" onLoad="placeElements()">
<DIV ID="text">Welcome</DIV>
<DIV ID="mindivTop"></DIV>
<DIV ID="mindivBottom"></DIV>
</BODY>
</HTML>
```

2. Save the document as X2.htm.

3. Open X2.htm in your browser.

4. Click anywhere on the window.

5. Refresh your browser, resize the window, and click again.

Explanation

Upon loading (or resizing) the window, the function placeElements() is called. This defines the top position (t) used to set the top position of the upper layer, and a position half way down the screen (b), which is used to position the top edge of the bottom layer:

```
t = 0;
b = document.body.clientHeight/2;
mindivTop.style.height = document.body.clientHeight/2;
mindivBottom.style.posTop = b;
mindivBottom.style.height = document.body.clientHeight/2;
```

To achieve this result, the window property clientHeight is used, thus b is set to the size of document.body (the window size) divided by two (/2). Similarly, the height of the style elements are each set to half of a window width. Notice that `clientWidth` also exists. In this case it is used to set the width (the max width) of the text layer:

```
text.style.width = document.body.clientWidth;
```

Upon clicking anywhere on the BODY, the function `start()` is called:

```
mindivTop.style.posTop = t=t-5;
   mindivBottom.style.posTop = b=b+5;
   if (b<=document.body.clientHeight)
   {
       setTimeout("start()",1);
   }
   else window.status="finished";
```

which simply subtracts five pixels from the value of the variable `t`, and adds five pixels to the value of the variable `b`. If `b` is smaller than or equal to the height of the screen, then `setTimeout` will call the function again after an interval of one millisecond, and again until the condition is met (the top of the bottom layer has met the bottom of the window), whereupon the status bar shows the message `"finished"`.

TIME-RELATED PROPERTIES OF THE WINDOW OBJECT

Property (setting)	Property (clearing)	Description
setTimeout	clearTimeout	Sets a one-time timer which invokes an expression (argument, function, etc.) after a delay of milliseconds.

Property (setting)	Property (clearing)	Description *(continued)*
setInterval	clearInterval	Starts a timer that continually invokes an expression (argument, function, etc.) in millisecond-defined intervals.

Example Y: Pre-loading Mouse-over Effects

The effect of having something happen when the mouse moves over an area is one everybody will have seen. For this Example you will need two GIF files called on.gif and off.gif. Here the size has been specified as width="13" height="21", but if you make yours a different size, remember to change the attributes in the HTML code.

1. Open your ASCII or HTML editor and type:

```
<HTML>
<head>
<title>Simple mouse over</title>
</head>
<body>
<a href="http://www.fbeedle.com"
onMouseOver="document.picture1.src='on.gif'"
onMouseOut="document.picture1.src='off.gif'">

<img src="off.gif" name="picture1" border="0" width="13"
height="21">Click here for Franklin Beedle
</a>
<p>
<a href="http://www.abfcontent.com"
```

```
onMouseOver="document.picture2.src='on.gif'"
onMouseOut="document.picture2.src='off.gif'">
<img src="off.gif" name="picture2" border="0" width="13"
height="21">Click here for ABF Content</a>
</body>
</HTML>
```

2. Save the document as Y1.htm.

3. Open Y1.htm in your browser and move the mouse over the images.

Explanation

Reference to the file off.gif is given within an anchor (A) tag:

```
<img src="off.gif" name="picture1" border="0" width="13"
height="21">
```

Notice that the image tag has been given a name. The width and height attributes are needed for Netscape compatibility, and the border is set to zero so as to avoid a blue (hyperlink color) border around the image. Thus, the document is loaded with off.gif shown. The A tags attributes include onMouseOver and onMouseOut:

```
<a href="http://www.fbeedle.com"
onMouseOver="document.picture1.src='on.gif'"
onMouseOut="document.picture1.src='off.gif'">
```

These use DOM dot syntax to refer to the image's source in the mouse's "over" and subsequent "off" states. Thus, when the mouse cursor position is over the IMG, the browser will check if it has the file "on.gif" cached or elsewhere, and, if not, will then request it from the server. Likewise, when the mouse cursor is moved off the IMG, then the browser will also request the file; but in this case it should already be in the cache (because it was called when the document loaded). The second link repeats the pattern of the first, but illustrates that the Over and Off states for the second link could easily refer to third and fourth image files.

As shown in Example O, arrays can be used to "pre-load" images, so the browser does not have to use time to go out and fetch the "Off" image.

1. To continue this example, re-open your ASCII or HTML editor and type:

```
<HTML>
<head>
<script language="JavaScript">
first = new Image();
first.src = "on.gif";
second = new Image();
second.src = "off.gif";
function imageIn(whichOne)
{
    document[whichOne].src=first.src;
}

function imageOut(whichOne)
{
    document[whichOne].src=second.src;
}
</script>
<title>Mouseover with pre-load</title>
</head>
<body>
<a href="http://www.fbeedle.com"
onMouseOver="imageIn('picture1')"
onMouseOut="imageOut('picture1')">
<img src="off.gif" name="picture1" border="0" width="13"
```

```
height="21"> Franklin Beedle</a>
<p>
<a href="http://www.abfcontent.com"
onMouseOver="imageIn('picture2')"
onMouseOut="imageOut('picture2')">
<img src="off.gif" name="picture2" border="0" width="13"
height="21"> ABFContent</a>
</body>
</HTML>
```

2. Save the document as Y2.htm.

3. Open Y2.htm in your browser.

Explanation

As in Y1.htm, the IMG elements are named:

```
<img src="off.gif" name="picture1" border="0" width="13"
height="21">
Franklin Beedle</a>
```

but now the mouse-over (and mouse-out) calls a function:

```
onMouseOver="imageIn('picture1')"
onMouseOut="imageOut('picture1')"
```

where the function's argument (picture1) is called:

```
function imageIn(whichOne)
{
document[whichOne].src=first.src;
```

and thus document.picture1.src = first.src, which in turn can be read from the array:

```
first.src = "on.gif";
```

Home Exercise 4: Pre-loaded Images, an Art Gallery

Make four GIF files, each about 100 by 100px. Make an HTML file containing JavaScript code in the HEAD and a FORM in the BODY. The FORM contains two or more buttons enabling the graphics to be shown in any order. The JavaScript contains an array, so all the graphics are loaded before clicking on the buttons. The images (several can be displayed at any one time) are changed using DOM dot syntax.

A suggestion to code is included in the web support, in a folder marked "homeX4."

Example Z: Timed Linked Graphical Sequence

It could be useful to have an image file replaced by another at set intervals, especially if a distinct and separate hyperlink could be "associated" to each one of the images. Such systems (e.g., banner adverts) normally rely on Java applets. However, combining arrays (Examples O and Y) together with the timer function (Example X) make this possible in JavaScript. For this example you will need four GIF files, preferably associated with four web site URLs.

1. Open your ASCII or HTML editor and type:

```
<HTML>
<HEAD>
<SCRIPT LANGUAGE="JavaScript">
index=0
// get the graphics

first = new Image();
second = new Image();
third = new Image();
fourth = new Image();
```

```
first.src = "logo1.gif";
second.src = "logo2.gif";
third.src = "logo3.gif";
fourth.src = "logo4.gif";

//Define the arrays

picture = new Array();
picture[0] = first.src;
picture[1] = second.src;
picture[2] = third.src;
picture[3] = fourth.src;

links = new Array();
links[0] = "http://www.fbeedle.com/"
links[1] = "ftp://ftp.adobe.com/"
links[2] = "mailto:info@fbeedle.com"
links[3] = "A.htm"

// links can be local, Internet or other HTTP protocols

elapse = new Array();
elapse[0] = 3;
elapse[1] = 5;
elapse[2] = 2;
elapse[3] = 9;

// changes the image at x milliseconds intervals
```

```
function changePicture()
{
    index++;
    if (index>(picture.length-1)) index=0
    document.sponsorlogo.src = picture[index];
    setTimeout("changePicture()",elapse[index]*1000);

    // multiplying by 1000 changes the interval to seconds
    // instead of milliseconds

}
</script>
</HEAD>
<BODY onLoad="changePicture()">
<CENTER>
<A HREF="javascript:window.location=links[index]"
onMouseOver="window.status='visit our sponsors';return true;"
onMouseOut="window.status='';return true;">
<IMG BORDER="0" width="100" height="100" SRC=""
NAME="sponsorlogo">
</A>
<BR>visit our sponsors
</CENTER>
</BODY>
</HTML>
```

2. Save the document as Z.htm.

3. Open Z.htm in your browser.

Upon BODY being loaded, the function `changePicture()` is called which sets the SRC attribute for the IMG element called `sponsorlogo` by pulling it out of the array:

```
document.sponsorlogo.src = picture[index];
```

After a set time interval:

```
setTimeout("changePicture()",elapse[index]*1000);
```

simply calls the function again, pulling in the next image. Associating the corresponding hyperlink (or `mailto` or whatever) is done in a parallel process. The IMG is in an Anchor element, whose HREF attribute is set to:

```
<A HREF="javascript:window.location=links[index]"
```

which puts the corresponding hyperlink into the code. Yet why does the hyperlink change in tact with the image? After all, `links[index]` is not timed at all! The answer lies in the array structure. Imagine the array as a table, so the first row will look like:

name	position	src	elapse	links
first	0	logo1.gif	3	http://www.fbeedle.com

So you can see that the link does not need to be timed separately, the "elapse" value also is valid for links, although not directly specified.

APPENDIX A

KEYWORD REFERENCE

ASCII American Standard Code for Information Interchange. A standard definition of character sets where each character is a direct representation of an 8-bit byte and therefore containing 255 characters (plus null). Slowly being replaced by 16-bit Unicode.

Attributes Specifications in HTML tags detailing properties, relating to style sheets, assigning functions or commands to execute, or other information.

DOM The Document Object Model, which regards all HTML elements as objects, specifies their relationship to each other (hierarchy), and defines which properties and methods these objects can have.

Dot Syntax A concatenation method and thus a means of defining an object by referring to its ancestors in the hierarchy (its parents and its parents' parents, etc., for example, document.form.input). Such notations are often referred to as collections.

ECMA European Computer Manufacturers Association, founded in 1961, and who, in 1997, announced a language standard for Internet scripting (ECMA-262) derived from Netscape's JavaScript specifications.

Event Handler Specific kinds of attributes assigning a JavaScript command or function which executes when the named event happens.

Function Collections of command and other code specifying an outcome. These can be standard functions inherently understood by the browser, like `getDay()`, or can be specially created by the web developer.

Hierarchy In an HTML page, objects exist in a hierarchical relationship to each other. For example, window is the parent of all other navigator objects. Location, history, and document are all children of a window at the same precedence level, but form, links, and anchors are children of a document.

Method A function assigned to an object. For example, `textstring.toUpperCase()` will return an upper case version of the text string contained within the variable `textstring`. In this case, the variable `textstring` is an object and the standard function `toUpperCase()` is a method.

MIME Multipurpose (or Multimedia) Internet Mail Extension. Defines the content type of a document, file, or message attachment; for example, image/gif or text/plain.

Object A construct having properties. These can be HTML elements as well as JavaScript variables, constants, and other constructs. The functions associated with objects are called methods. The properties of an object are accessed using dot syntax: `objectName.propertyName`, where both object and property names are case sensitive.

Operator Perform a function or operation on one or more operands or variables. Operators are divided into two classes; binary and unary. Binary operators (like addition, a + b) need two operands, whereas unary operators (like incrementation, a ++) require only one.

Property Used to describe an object. A property can be defined by assigning it a value, but other properties contain constants—values that never change.

APPENDIX B

OVERVIEW OF OBJECTS

To view or manipulate the state of an object requires the use of its properties and methods. Objects may also be properties of another object.

Object	Description
anchors	A read-only object set in HTML using <A> tags. A property of `document`. To determine how many anchors there are in a document, the length property is used: `document.anchors.length`
button	A form element (always defined in <FORM> tags) used to perform an action. A property of form: Properties: name, value. Method: click. Event handler: onClick.
checkbox	A form element (always defined in <FORM> tags) input field. A property of form: Properties: checked, defaultChecked, name, value. Method: click. Event handler: onClick.
date	Starts at 01.01.1970. Numerical representations begin with zero (i.e., January=0, December=11). Properties: none. Methods: getDate, getDay, getHours, getMinutes, getMonth, detSeconds, getTime, getTimezoneOffset, getYear, parse, setDate, setHours, setMinutes, setMonth, setSeconds, setTime, setYear, toGMTString, toLocaleString, toString.
document	An object created when a page is loaded and containing properties contained in the <BODY> tags.

Object	Description *(continued)*
	Properties: alinkColor, anchors, bgColor, cookie, fgColor, forms, lastModified, linkColor, links, location, referrer, title, vlinkColor. Method: clear, close, open, write, writeln. Event handler: onLoad, onUnLoad.
elements	An array of <FORM> elements in source order. Property: length.
form	Each form in a document is a separate and distinct object. If the first form was named form1, then it can be referenced as either document.form1 or as document.form[0]. Note that data from forms is always sent as strings. Properties: action, elements, encoding, forms, method, name, target. Method: submit. Event handler: onSubmit.
frame	Each frame is a window object as defined in the <FRAMESET> tags. All subdocuments are children of the parent, so if a frame contains the SRC and NAME attributes then it can be identified using parent.frameName. Properties: defaultStatus, frames, parent, self, status, top, window. Methods: setTimeout, clearTimeout.
hidden	An invisible input text object used to pass name/value pairs. A property of form. Properties: cookie, defaultValue, name, value.

history	Derived from the GO menu, history contains URL information about visited pages. A property of document. Property: length. Methods: back, forward, go.
link	A location object and property of document. Properties: hash, host, hostname, href, length, pathname, port, protocol, search, target. Method: link. Event handlers: onClick, onMouseOver.
location	Contains the URL information for the current document. Properties: hash, host, hostname, href, length, pathname, port, protocol, search, target.
math	Contains properties for mathematical constants (for example the value of pi is accessed by Math.pi) and standard trigonometrical (in radians!), logarithmic, and exponential methods for functions. Properties: E, LN10, LN2, PI, SQRT1_2, SQRT2. Methods: abs, acos, asin, atan, ceil, cos, exp, floor, log, max, min, pow, random, round, sin, sqrt, tan.
navigator	Contains information on the client browser. Properties: appName, appCodeName, appVersion, userAgent.
option	Objects within <FORM> tags representing option buttons. Properties: checked, defaultChecked, index, length, name, value. Method: click. Event handler: onClick.

Object	Description *(continued)*
password	Input in <FORM> field which is masked when entered. Properties: defaultValue, name, value. Methods: focus, blur, select.
reset	Resets all form values to their default values. Properties: name, value. Method: click. Event handler: onClick.
select	A selection or scrolling list enabling one or more choices to be made. Properties: length, name, options, selectedIndex (options also contains; defaultSelected, index, selected, text, value). Methods: blur, focus. Event handlers: onBlur, onChange, onFocus.
string	A series of characters defined by single (') or double (") quotes. Property: length. Methods: anchor, big, blink, bold, charAt, fixed, fontColor, fontSize, indexOf, italics, lastIndexOf, link, small, strike, sub, substring, sup, toLowerCase, toUpperCase.
submit	Causes a form to be submitted to the program specified by the Action property. It always loads a new page (the default value being the same page again). Properties: name, value. Method: click. Event handler: onClick.

text	A form input field accepting either characters or numbers. Text objects can be updated by assigning new contents to their values. Properties: defaultValue, name, value. Methods: focus, blur, select. Event handlers: onBlur, onChange, onFocus, onSelect.
textarea	Similar to text, with the addition of multiple lines. Properties: defaultValue, name, value. Methods: focus, blur, select. Event handlers: onBlur, onChange, onFocus, onSelect.

window	Object created by navigator when a page is loaded containing properties appertaining to the whole window. It is the top-level object for each document, location, and history object. The window's name does not need to be referenced; for example, there is no difference between:
	    status("welcome")
	    window.status("welcome")
	New windows are created using the open method:
	    aNewWindow = window.open
	The variable name is used to refer to the window's properties and methods:
	    aNewWindow = window.open("URL","name",["features"])
	The window name is used in the target argument of a form or anchor.
	Properties: defaultStatus, frames, parent, self, status, top, window.
	Methods: alert, close, confirm, open, prompt, setTimeout, clearTimeout.
	Event handlers: onLoad, onUnload.

APPENDIX C

OVERVIEW OF METHODS

Methods are functions and procedures used to perform an operation on an object, a variable, or a constant. With few exceptions (built-in functions), methods must be used with an object, and the trailing brackets () are required, even if they do not contain an argument, e.g.:

```
object.method()
```

Method	Description
abs	Returns the absolute value of an argument; `document.write(Math.abs(-4));` returns 4.
acos	Returns the arc cosine (from 0 to Pi radians) of arguments between 1 and -1. Returns 0 if outside this valid range.
alert	Displays an Alert dialog box with an OK button and user-defined message. The client must click on OK before continuing.
anchor	Used with write or writeln (write line) methods, anchor creates and displays a hypertext target, where textString represents what the client sees and anchorName is the <a name = attribute: `textString.anchor(anchorName)`
asin	Returns the arc sine between -Pi/2 and Pi/2 radians of numbers between -1 and 1.
atan	Returns the arc tangent between -Pi/2 and Pi/2 radians of numbers between -1 and 1.
back	Recalls the previous URL from the history list. This is functionally the same as: `history.go(-1)`

big	Formats an object by encasing it in <BIG> tags:
	`var message="welcome"`
	`document.write(message.big());`

Method	Description *(continued)*

blink	Reminiscent of the defunct Netscape tag <BLINK>:
	`var message="welcome"`
	`document.write(message.blink());`

blur	Removes focus from a specified FORM element

bold	Similar to big:
	`var message="welcome"`
	`document.write(message.bold());`

ceil	Method of Math, returning a "ceiling" value, the smallest integer greater than or equal to its argument: `Math.ceil(1.7)` returns 2.

charAt	Returns the character from a string at the position specified in the argument:
	`var message="welcome"`
	`document.write(message.charAt(4));`
	returns c.

clear	Clears the content of a window.
clearTimeout	Clears a Timeout, but only by reference to the Timeout's name.
click	Simulates a mouse click.
close	Used on window, closes that window. Used on document it closes and displays the output, stops winsock animations, and writes "Document: Done" in the status bar.

confirm	Displays a Confirm box containing OK and Cancel buttons.
cos	Returns the cosine of an angle's size (in radians).
escape	Returns the ASCII code of its argument based on ISO-Latin-1.

eval	Takes string or numeric data, evaluates it, and attempts to convert it to the relevant data type:
	`var x = 10`
	`var y = "20"`
	`document.write(eval("x + y"))`
	Useful in, e.g., converting dates sent by forms.

exp	Returns e (Eulers constant) to the power of the argument. Useful in computing natural logarithms.
floor	Returns the integer less than or equal to its argument, e.g.: `Math.floor(1.7)` returns 1.
focus	Gives a specific form element focus (i.e., the cursor on that element)
fontcolor	Formats a string to a specific color.
fontsize	Formats a string to a specific absolute size, unless <BASFONT> has been specified, in which case the size change is relative.
forward	Loads the next document on the URL history list.
getDate	Returns the day of the month as an integer between 1 and 31.

Method	Description *(continued)*
getDay	Returns the day of the week as an integer between zero (Sunday) and 6 (Saturday).
getHours	Returns the hour of the day from zero (midnight) to 23.
getMinutes	Returns minutes from zero to 59.
getMonth	Returns the month from zero (January) to 11 (December).
getSeconds	Returns seconds from zero to 59.
getTime	Returns an integer representing the number of milliseconds since midnight 01.01.1970.
getTimezoneOffset	Returns the difference in minutes between the client PC and Greenwich Mean Time (GMT).
getYear	Returns the year of the date object minus 1900, i.e., 1998 returns as 98.
go	Loads a document specified in the history list by URL or current position on history list.
indexOf	Returns the location of a specified character or string starting from a specified location. The first character of the string searched is number zero and the last is "length-1". The syntax is: stringName.indexOf([character ǀ string], [startingPoint])
isNaN	Returns true if the argument "is Not a Number." Used only on Unix platforms.

italics	Similar to big:

```
var message="welcome"
document.write(message.italics());
```

lastIndexOf	Returns the location of a specified character or string starting backwards from a specified location or from the end.
link	Creates a hyperlink to a URL by defining the link text and using the URL defined in HREF.
log	Returns the natural logarithm of a number.
max	Returns the greater of its two arguments:

```
Math.max(1, 2)
```
Returns 2.

min	Returns the lesser of its two arguments:

```
Math.max(1, 2)
```
Returns 1.

open	Used on document, open will clear any document already in the target window and open a stream to output the write or writeln methods.

Used on window, open will open a new blank window. If the URL argument is used, then the URL will be loaded into the blank window. Characteristics of the new window can be defined by a comma-separated list of options where =1 or =yes enables, and =0 or =no disables. The list includes toolbar, location, directories, status, menubar, scrollbars, resizable, copyhistory, width, and height.

147

Method	Description *(continued)*
parse	Takes a date string (e.g., Nov 19, 1995) and returns the number of milliseconds since midnight 01.01.1970.
parseFloat	Returns a floating-point number of an argument. If the first character is not valid in the context, then it returns 0 (on Windows platform) or NaN (on other platforms).
pow	Returns a base raised to exponent.
prompt	Displays a Prompt dialog box containing default or specified values.
random	Returns a pseudo-random number.
round	Returns a decimal (floating-point) rounded up to the next highest integer.
select	Selects the input area of a specified form element and positions the cursor for client input.
setDate	Sets the day of the month.
setHours	Sets the hour of the current time.
setMinutes	Sets the minutes of the current time.
setMonth	Sets the month with an integer from 0 (January) to 11 (December).
setSeconds	Sets the seconds of the current time.
setTime	Sets the value of a Date object.
setTimeout	Evaluates an expression after a one-time given interval.

setYear	Sets the year of the current date.
sin	Returns the sine of an argument (the size of an angle expressed in radians).

small	Similar to big:
	
	```var message="welcome"```
	```document.write(message.small());```

sqrt	Returns the square root of a positive number. Returns 0 if the argument is invalid.

strike	Similar to big:
	
	```var message="welcome"```
	```document.write(message.strike());```

sub	Similar to big:
	
	```var message="welcome"```
	```document.write(message.sub());```

submit	Performs the same action as clicking the submit button.
substring	Returns a subset of a string object based on two indices, from the smallest to the largest.

sup	Similar to big:
	
	```var message="welcome"```
	```document.write(message.sup());```

tan	Returns the tangent of an argument (the size of an angle expressed in radians).
toGMTString	Converts a date object to a string using GMT.

Method	Description *(continued)*
toLocaleString	Converts a date object to a string using local conventions.
toLowerCase	Converts all characters in a string to lower case.
toString	Converts date or location objects to a string.
toUpperCase	Converts all characters in a string to upper case (capital letters).
unEscape	Used to reconvert strings subjected to Escape.
UTC	A constant, used as: `Date.UTC()` returning the number of milliseconds since midnight 01.01.1970.
write	Writes one or more lines to a document, but needs ` ` or /n characters to add new lines or line breaks.
writeln	Writes one or more lines to a document followed by a new line.

APPENDIX D

OVERVIEW OF PROPERTIES

Property	Description
action	Destination URL for form submitted data.

alinkColor	The color of an active link. Note the lack of a pound (#) sign if hexadecimal notation is used:
	`document.alinkColor="silver"`
	`document.alinkColor="C0C0C0"`

anchors	An array of all defined anchors.
appCodeName	Returns a read-only string containing the browser's code name.
appName	Returns a read-only string containing the browser's name.

Property	Description *(continued)*
appVersion	Returns a read-only string containing the browser's version in the format "releaseNumber(platform; country).

bgColor	The background color. Note the lack of a pound (#) sign even when the hexadecimal form is used:
	`document.bgColor="silver"`
	`document.bgColor="C0C0C0"`

checked	A Boolean value (true or false) indicating if a checkbox or radio button is checked.
cookie	String value stored in a client-side file.
defaultChecked	A Boolean value (true or false) indicating whether a checkbox or radio button is checked by default.
defaultSelected	A Boolean value (true or false) indicating whether a form element is checked by default.
defaultStatus	Default message in the status bar.
defaultValue	The initial contents of hidden, password, text, textarea, and string form elements.
E	Eulers constant (2.7182818285).
elements	An array of objects containing form elements in HTML source order.
encoding	Returns a string reflecting the MIME type.

fgColor	The foreground color. Note the lack of a pound (#) sign if the hexadecimal form is used:
	`document.fgColor="silver"`
	`document.fgColor="C0C0C0"`

forms	An array object corresponding to named forms in their HTML source order.
frames	An array of objects corresponding to child frame windows created using the <FRAMESET> tag. The number of frames is obtained using the length property.
hash	Returns a string with the portion of an URL beginning with a pound (#) sign (anchor to bookmark). Returns an error if no pound character is found.
host	Returns a string formed by combining the hostname and port properties of a URL: `location.host="www.fbeedle.com:80"` A useful way of changing port number.
hostname	Returns (or changes) a string containing the domain name or IP address of a URL.
href	Returns a string of the entire URL.
index	Returns the index of an option in a select element with 0 as the first item.
lastModified	Returns a read-only string containing the date at which the file attributes indicate it was last modified.

Property	Description *(continued)*
length	An integer reflecting a length or size-related property of an object.

linkColor	The color of a link. Note the lack of a pound (#) sign if the hexadecimal form is used:
	`document.linkColor="silver"`
	`document.linkColor="C0C0C0"`

links	An array representing all link objects as defined in HTML using <a href="">.
LN2	A constant representing the natural logarithm of 2 (approximately 0.693).
LN10	A constant representing the natural logarithm of 10 (approximately 2.302).
location	Returns a read-only string with the URL of the current document. Should not be confused with the location object.
LOG2E	A constant representing the base 2 logarithm of E (approximately 1.442).
LOG10E	A constant representing the base 10 logarithm of E (approximately 0.434).

method	Reflects the method attribute of an HTML form field:
	`function getMethod(formObj){`
	`return formObj.method}`
	would return the current method value (GET or POST)

while:
```
function setMethod(formObj.newMethod) {
formObj.method = newMethod}
```
would set the method to the contents of the variable newMethod.

name   Returns a string containing the name attribute of an object. Note that this is not the on-screen, client-visible name on buttons, etc.

options   An array of option objects created by a SELECT form element, with the first being 0.

parent   Refers to the calling document in the current frame created by FRAMESET. This allows writing to other documents in the same frameset, for example in a frameset consisting of a halved screen left and right, then the document in right could contain:
```
parent.left.document.write("text from right")
```

pathname   Returns the path portion of a URL.

PI   Returns the value of Pi (the ratio of the circumference of a circle to its diameter), approx. 3.1415927.

port   Returns the port number of a URL.

protocol   Returns a string containing the initial portion of an URL up to and including the colon (:) character, e.g.:
http:
ftp:

Property	Description *(continued)*
	mailto:
	telenet:
referrer	Returns a read-only URL of the document that called the current document.
search	Returns a string containing any query information appended to an URL.
selected	Returns a Boolian value (true or false) indicating the current state of an OPTION in a SELECT element.
selectedIndex	Returns an integer specifying the index of a selected item.
self	Refers to the current window or form. Useful in exceptions where <BASE TARGET=""> is specified in HTML.
SQRT1_2	Returns the square root of ½ (the inverse of the square root of 2, approx. 0.707).
SQRT2	Returns the square root of 2 (approx. 1.414).
status	Specifies a property or transient message to display in the status bar at the bottom of the window.
target	A string specifying the name of a window for responses to be posted to after a form submission, or, if in connection with a hyperlink, a string specifying the name of the window showing the linked document.
text	Returns the value of text within OPTION tags in a SELECT element.

title	Returns the read-only value set within HTML title tags. Returns "null" if TITLE is lacking.
top	The topmost window.
userAgent	Header sent as part of HTTP, similar to appVersion.
value	The value of an INPUT object: the client-visible text on a button; "on" or "off" for a checkbox; the value of radio buttons; strings within hidden and text fields; contents of textarea and select.
vlinkColor	The color of a visited link. Note the lack of a pound (#) sign if hexadecimal notation is used: `document.vlinkColor="silver"` `document.vlinkColor="C0C0C0"`
window	A synonym for the current window to remove ambiguity between the window object and any form object having the same name. Most programmers avoid this and prefer to use "self."

APPENDIX E

FURTHER INFORMATION ON THE INTERNET

Microsoft:

msdn.microsoft.com/downloads/samples/internet/default.asp

Netscape:

developer.netscape.com

Certification:

inter-col.net/fbeedle.htm

Freebies:

There are hundreds of other private web sites offering free tutorials, tips, code stumps, and the like. The following are just a few of the classic ones. By visiting these you will find links to many others:

htmlgoodies.earthweb.com
www.cotse.com
webdeveloper.com
javascript.com
www.webreference.com/

APPENDIX F

FAQS

An "Afterword" to *DHTML: Learning by Example*, along with a list of frequently asked questions (FAQs), is kept updated on the publisher's web site (**www.fbeedle.com**).

Question	Comment
I want to date-mark my HTML files so people can see when the last update was. Is there an automatic way of doing this?	The best way is to have an `onLoad` event handler in the BODY statement calling a function, which in turn contains: `document.write("updated on " + document.lastModified)` or similar.

How can I put page breaks in HTML sides?	You do that by setting up a class of page breaks. You can set up the class on any HTML command, but I think the best method is to set up the class within a BR or P tags. That way there's some white space where the page can break. Here's a look at the format (this will sit between your flags):
	`<STYLE TYPE="text/css"> P.breakhere`
	`{page-break-before: always} </STYLE>`
	This then will be the activator for the page break:
	`<P CLASS="breakhere">`
	    You can set up as many different classes as you'd like as long as you keep following the same format as above (or similar).

I'm having trouble with pop-up boxes. How do I open new windows of a certain size? At the moment I'm using HTML code `<target="_blank">` and trying to specify the new window's size in the new HTML document.	Older browsers will not recognize the resize method, so use open instead. Write a function in HEAD thus:
	`function box(URL)`
	`{window.open(URL,'box','menubar=yes,status=no,`
	`resizable=yes,scrollbars=yes,width=30,height=20')}`
	and call it using:
	`<a href="javascript:box("file.htm')"> open file</a>`
	    But remember you can call the function box only once, meaning you can only have one new window open at a time. If you want

Question	Comment (*continued*)
	several, you will have to repeat the function (name it box2) and call it using: `<a href="javascript:box2("file2.htm")">`

Apparently some people keep visiting HTML files which should properly be viewed in frames. Is there a way to fix this?	If your visitors are in a frame, then you can use location, like:
	`parent.contents.location="menu.htm"`
	but if your visitors are totally outside of the frame, then a little more force has to be used. The most elegant way is to use an IF statement to compare self to parent and use the outcome to refresh to a different URL:
	`if (self==parent){`
	`document.write("<meta HTTP-EQUIV=Refresh CONTENT=1;`
	`URL=http://www.fbeedle.com target=_top>')};`
	Note that this code must be in HEAD.

Is there any way I can "count down" a clock on a page?	Look at the following code. Calling startclock sets a loop running that clears timeout, displays the current time, and sets timeout to re-display the time in two seconds. Use it as inspiration (it should contain all the ingredients you need), but find your own answers.
	`var timerID=null;`
	`var timerRunning=false;`
	`function stopclock()`
	`{if(timerRunning) clearTimeout(timerID);`
	`timerRunning=false;}`
	`function startclock(){`
	`stopclock();`
	`showtime();}`

```
function showtime(){
var now=new Date();
document.clock.face.value=timeValue;
timerID=setTimeout("showtime()", 2000);
timerRunning=true;}
```

Can I use a Prompt box in connection with a hyperlink to ask visitors if they really want to visit that link?

Of course, but perhaps a Confirm box is better. Open a new window to make it easy for your visitor to return:

```
If (confirm("are u sure") {
sesame = window.open("http://www.fbeedle.com",
"books")}
```

What is VBS ?

VBS stands for Visual Basic Script and is not used client-side on the Internet. VBS should not be confused with VBScript.

VBS can start, use, and shut down PC applications without client (user) knowledge. If you receive uninvited VBS files (the extension is vbs; e.g. fileName.vbs) by mail or embedded in HTML files, then you should immediately delete them as they can easily be malicious programs or viruses.

I cannot call functions in external files.

The newer browsers, like MS Internet Explorer 5.5 and Netscape 6, do not wait to read in whole external files, so:

```
<SCRIPT SRC="FileWithFunctionIn.js">
externalfunction()
</script>
```

may well not work in these browsers. The work-around is to divide them such that the browser pauses and reads in the code before continuing to the next block:

Question	Comment (*continued*)

	``html
	<SCRIPT SRC="FileWithFunctionIn.js">
	</script>
	<SCRIPT language="JavaScript">
	externalfunction()
	</script>
	``

Is there any way of getting the Object tag to work in Netscape?	Not precisely, but you can combine the Object and Embed tags:
	``html
	<object classid="" height="" width="">
	<!-- parameters here -->
	<embed src="" height="" width="">
	<noembed>
	<img src="default.gif">
	</noembed>
	</embed>
	</object>
	``
	So, if neither the Object tag nor the Embed tag works in that browser, then at the least a default image is shown instead.

In Example R, the classID registry value for ActiveX was given. Are there any other useful classIDs?	Sure:
	ActiveX:
	`CLASSID="CLSID:333C7BC4-460F-11D0-BC04-0080C7055A83"`
	Flash:
	`CLASSID="CLSID:D27CDB6E-AE6D-11cf-96B8-444553540000"`
	Shockwave:
	`CLASSID="CLSID:166B1BCA-3F9C-11cf-8075-444553540000"`
	RealMedia:
	`CLASSID="CLSID:CFCDAA03-8BE4-11cf-B84B-0020AFBBCCFA"`

INDEX